31 Days

of Power

Learning to Live in Spiritual Victory

Ruth Myers

with Warren Myers

MULTNOMAH
BOOKS

THIRTY-ONE DAYS OF POWER

Chapter epigraphs in Part II are from the hymns "We Rest on Thee" by Edith G. Cherry and "A Mighty Fortress Is Our God" by Martin Luther.

Trade Paperback ISBN 978-1-60142-338-2
eBook ISBN 978-0-307-56333-0

Published in the United States by Multnomah, an imprint of the Crown Publishing Group, a division of Penguin Random House LLC, New York.

MULTNOMAH® and its mountain colophon are registered trademarks of Penguin Random House LLC.

Library of Congress Cataloging-in-Publication Data
Myers, Ruth.
    31 days of power / by Ruth Myers with Warren Myers
        p. cm.
    1. Spiritual warfare—Prayer-books and devotions—English. 2. Devotional calendars. I. Title.
BV4509.M94 2003
235'.4—dc22

2003016329

Printed in the United States of America
2018

10 9 8 7 6

Contents

PART II

THE DYNAMICS OF SPIRITUAL WARFARE

THIS IS WAR

The fighting bridges all of time. The battles began in ages past and are destined to keep growing in intensity until Jesus returns to reign over all the earth.

This is the supremely ultimate war, the conflict overarching all others. It is God's war against Satan and his subordinates. And in this war, God has called you and me to be His soldiers. What a privilege!

And yet—so challenging! And sometimes scary.

Our battle isn't against people with human bodies, but against invisible spiritual enemies who bitterly oppose us—vicious, murderous warriors in Satan's army. We face a ruthless foe who prowls about like a lion, grimly committed to defeat and devour us. As part of the conflict, we must also confront this world's system with its subtle corruptions and never-ending pressures, while we contend as well with our own indwelling sin which so easily ensnares us. How overmatched and endangered our faith can seem at times!

But we know God's promise: The strength He offers us is so overpowering that we can be not only conquerors but "more than conquerors"..."we overwhelmingly conquer" through our Father who loves us (Romans 8:37, NKJV, NASB). We read that He "gives us the victory through our Lord Jesus Christ," not only victory over eternal spiritual death but victory to live and reign as kings in this life (1 Corinthians 15:57; Romans 5:17).

But how can this be real in our own experience? How can we actually live each day in the dynamic triumph God offers us in Christ?

The goal of this book is to help you answer that question for yourself in God's presence through prayer and praise, and through an overview of critical truths from God's Word concerning the power and victory that are ours. I want to help you develop a balanced and positive approach to your spiritual warfare, an approach that will increase your skill in resisting Satan's purposes and promoting those of our triumphant Lord. Another goal is to help you not to honor Satan through being preoccupied with him and his helpers.

This Book's Arrangement

Any form of sincere, believing prayer will direct God's power into our lives and situations, and this is especially true of prayer blended with praise. Part I in this book includes thirty-one daily portions of prayer and praise. These will help you reflect and build on the rich treasures of truth God has revealed regarding spiritual conflict and triumph.

These days of prayer and praise are designed to help you lift your soul to God with greater freedom to sense His presence and count on His power. I pray that this will fortify you to overcome Satan in new ways, both in your life and in the lives of others.

Meanwhile, as we continue running into our own skirmishes and struggles—for all of life is a part of the great overarching spiritual conflict—we do well to ask ourselves again and again, *What is this war all about? Why am I wrestling, agonizing, in this current battle?* To help you keep this big picture in focus, in Part II you'll journey through foundational truths in Scripture about spiritual warfare and victory. These truths can guide you in keeping your response to this battle positive rather than negative—in focusing chiefly on God rather than on Satan.

The truths in this book have been tested for years, for decades. I've found them to be indeed reliable in my personal needs and struggles. And I've seen them help others defeat the powers of darkness through our Lord Jesus Christ—through focusing on His grace and glory as the one true Victor and Conqueror.

These truths flow from digging into God's Word—from daily searching it, soaking in its truths, and meditating with praise on Jesus as Victor. During my years as a widow in the 1960s, I began to put some of these truths on paper in a study called "Jesus Is Victor." Later, my second husband Warren and I did considerable searching into the Scriptures on the subjects of spiritual warfare and strategic prayer. We further developed and used these truths during our decades as missionaries in Asia, including Warren's six years with cancer before the Lord called him Home in 2001.

We learned, for example, that warfare against Satan is far more than the obvious battles against demonic oppression, active demonism, Satan worship, and the occult. In every situation of our lives—in times of obvious blessing or in times of trial, large or small—

God has a purpose in mind, and so does Satan.

Basically, Satan always wants to bring about the opposite of what God has in mind. God wants to draw us closer to Himself; Satan wants to draw us away. God wants to strengthen our faith; Satan wants to weaken it, bringing in doubt and destruction. God wants to purify our character; Satan wants to corrupt it. God wants to liberate us from worldly values; Satan wants to entangle us, to whet our appetite for the things that grieve God and dilute our passion to honor Him and please Him. God wants to increase our love for people and our readiness to forgive offenses; Satan wants to nurture bitterness and resentment.

So our whole life is part of the battle between God and Satan.

We also learned that the primary goal of our warfare is not to defeat Satan. Our chief goal as soldiers of the King is to further God's gracious and glorious purposes in this world—to help fulfill His longing for a vast family of children conformed to the image of His Son. In pursuing this goal, we must resist Satan and bring Christ's power to bear against him as he seeks to frustrate our Father's purposes. But even as we resist him, even as we wrestle with his invisible powers, we're to be preoccupied not with our enemy but with our victorious Lord and His purposes.

In this battle, one main task is to pray. Another is to share the good news of the reconciled life and the victorious life. Whether in large or small ways, we're to work with our Father as He rescues people from the domain of darkness and transfers them into the kingdom of His beloved Son (Colossians 1:13). Then we can watch for opportunities to help new citizens of the kingdom adjust their lives to the ways of their new spiritual culture, and to equip them for their part in the battle.

What about casting out demons? This is an important ministry, and I pray that God will continue to raise up mature believers equipped to help demonized people find deliverance. But this is not our main task. I see Paul as our model in this. His main thrust was proclaiming the gospel and building up those who had come to Christ, and now and then he cast out demons.

In all our warfare, our chief focus should be on God and His gracious purposes, not on Satan and demons and their evil strategies. We need to know what God tells us about our enemy and his methods, and we must learn to stand against his purposes. But far more, we need to grow in our knowledge of God and of His directions for our warfare. This book will guide you as you seek to do this more effectively and more constantly.

By no means am I an expert on spiritual warfare. I have learned much—and still have much to learn. In my years of missionary service I was never actually in the front lines of an initial thrust into resistant enemy territory. But especially in Asia, Warren and I gleaned a lot from frontline soldiers about spiritual warfare, including such things as demon expulsion and the occult. This book doesn't attempt to cover thoroughly all the ways Satan seeks to invade people's lives. Rather it seeks to lead you into positive ways that you can overcome him.

I pray that God will use what is shared in these pages to deepen your experience of the One through whom we can win overwhelming victories. We can truly say with confidence, "Through God we will do valiantly, for it is He who shall tread down our enemies" (Psalm 60:12, NKJV).

THIRTY-ONE DAYS OF POWER

DAY
1

COMMANDER OF VICTORIES

Father in heaven, I lift up my heart to You as the gracious and almighty Ruler of all things everywhere. How grateful I am that You have given us the powerful weapons of prayer and praise to help win victories over our spiritual enemies.

Thank You that prayer and praise give me constant opportunities to be on active duty in the spiritual war that surrounds us. How glad I am, my King and my God, that through prayer I can influence You to command victories near and far—in my own life and service, in the lives of those around me, and in those laboring for You in the far corners of the earth. Through prayer and praise I can help them be strong in faith and bold in their witness even when Satan seeks to sift them as wheat. What a privilege this is!

PSALM 44:4; LUKE 22:31–32

I worship You as our supreme Ruler, sovereign over all. You are all-powerful and all-wise. You are exalted far above all powers and rulers, both good and evil, visible and invisible. I praise You that You reign over all, with never the slightest alarm about the powers of evil, for Your throne is never threatened.

1 Chronicles 29:11–12

Thank You that You are infinitely greater than that old serpent, the devil, who started this centuries-long war against You, trying to usurp Your authority and power. I rejoice that ages ago You cast him out of Your headquarters in heaven. And You are constantly working all things according to the counsel of Your will, including everything regarding our enemy. You never look back and say "Oops, I shouldn't have allowed Satan to do that." Century after century he operates only under You and in ultimate subjection to Your purposes.

Revelation 12:9; Ephesians 1:11

So I take my stand in You as the One who is sovereign over all evil influences. I count on You as a shield around me. I stand against the works of the flesh and the enticements of the world that so easily distract me and hinder my prayers. I choose to put off the filthy clothes of fleshly living—the selfishness, the lust, the distrust, the neglect of my privilege of prayer. As Your chosen child, I put on the beautiful garments You've provided through the life of Christ in me. I give You thanks for my weakness, and I glory in the truth that Your strength is made perfect in weakness—that out of my weakness You are making me strong.

1 JOHN 2:15–17; 2 CORINTHIANS 12:9

VICTORY DESIGN

How I praise You, Ruler of the ages, that You've brought me into the stream of Your purposes—into Your glorious plan. You've taught me to yield all my allegiance to You as my King. And You've enlisted me into Your army to join Your people in doing battle under Your sovereign rule. You're counting on all Your children to be involved in this ages-long battle to defeat Satan, turning people from his kingdom to Yours—"to open their eyes so that they may turn from darkness to light and from the dominion of Satan to God." So I rejoice and pray, focusing on Your unparalleled power and Your glorious eternal plans.

2 TIMOTHY 2:3; 1 TIMOTHY 4:12; ACTS 26:18

You are the living Rock, solid and unshakable. Your glorious power surrounds me, overshadows me, and prepares the way before me. You are my Strength and Shield, my Saving Defense and Refuge, my Sure Footing, and my all-sufficient God who is enough. You make me steadfast and immovable! I worship You as the greatest, most awesome of all beings—more impressive, more powerful than anything on earth. You are exalted high above any hindrances or adversaries that loom large in my life right now, whether in my personality or my present circumstances or my future.

DEUTERONOMY 32:4; PSALM 28:7; 1 CORINTHIANS 15:58

You, Lord God, are Yahweh Most High, the great King over all the earth, You are the Overcomer, the almighty Conqueror, able to win overwhelming victories. And You are my sanctuary, the holy, secluded, safe place where I can enter and be at rest in Your strength. Thank You that I can conquer because I trust in You!

PSALM 97:9; 47:2–3; 62:7; 2 CHRONICLES 13:18

I exult that You are seated in the heavenlies, high above all enemy powers, and I am seated with You! So in my battles with Satan I can come at him from above. I shout to You with a voice of joy and triumph, for You're the One who subdues the enemy under my feet.

EPHESIANS 1:20–22; 2:6; PSALM 47:1, 3

For everything I need, what a privilege it is to go right to the top—to the supreme Authority, the highest

Ruler, who is all-powerful and all-loving—to the One who deeply cares about my well-being and loves me with a perfect love. To the best of my knowledge, I surrender wholly to You. And I trust You to continue Your gracious work of cleansing and transforming my life—of sanctifying me wholly, body, soul, and spirit.

ROMANS 12:1; 1 THESSALONIANS 5:23

D A Y
3

GREATER

Father, I lift my heart in worship, for You are the great and awesome God. I ascribe to You glory and strength; I give to You the glory that You deserve; I worship You in the beauty of holiness.

PSALM 29:1–2

I stand in awe of You, for Your voice is powerful. You are the One who speaks and it is done, as You demonstrated when You created the universe. Thank You for Your voice of authority which terrifies our enemies as we rely on You, and for the blows of Your arm which they cannot escape.

PSALMS 33:8–10; 2:5; 98:1

How great and mighty You are, infinitely more powerful than any human might. You are immeasurably stronger than all military forces and all weapons, even the most devastating. Your might is unlimited, unbounded, far beyond anything we can imagine. You are well able to destroy all the schemes and plots and works of Satan. And Your

power is a loving power, able to turn into blessing
even the worst that Satan does.

2 CHRONICLES 20:6; PSALM 62:11–12

How unnerving it is, Lord, to see the crafty
ways Satan tries to weaken our faith and destroy our
walk with You. But I worship You as the strongest
Strong One. You are the Lord of hosts—of vast
spiritual armies, infinitely greater than Satan and his
legions of evil spirits. Thank You that praising and
worshiping You stimulates my faith and makes my
spiritual enemies cringe in defeat.

JOB 9:19; ISAIAH 2:12

You are the living God, the God of mighty
victories, the God of both heaven and earth. You are
enthroned higher than the highest angels. And You
alone are God of all the kingdoms of the earth. I
count on You to work in this world in ways that will
hasten Your purposes and cause countless people to
trust Christ as their Savior and Lord.

JEREMIAH 10:10; PSALM 57:5

Thank You for Christ's promise that those who
believe in Him would do even greater works than He
did in His ministry on earth. In this continuing war
against Satan, enable me to fulfill the purposes You
have for me, both small and great—through prayer,

through using my spiritual gifts, and through being a witness for You to unbelievers as well as to people who already know You.

JOHN 14:12

    I pray especially about the following needs and opportunities, both near and far:

_____

_____

_____

_____

_____

_____

    To You, Father, the only God our Savior, through Jesus Christ our Lord, be glory and majesty, dominion and authority, both now and forever. Amen.

JUDE 1:25

THE POWER OF
HIS GOODNESS

How glad I am, Lord, that the basic secret for overcoming our enemy is simply knowing You in a vital and deepening relationship. Thank You that the more I let You meet my deep needs, the less vulnerable I am to temptation and the stronger I am to do Your will.

ACTS 20:32; 2 PETER 1:3–4; 3:18

I praise You that You are exalted high above all. You're the Ruler over everything and everyone. This would be a terrifying thought if You were evil, or if You had evil streaks in Your nature. But how assuring it is to know that You are altogether holy and righteous and loving—a wise God who knows all things and always wills the best for us. I honor You for being totally good in Your character, and I'm so glad that Your will for us is also totally good. You always have the best purposes in mind for whatever You bring into our lives or allow to happen. What stability we have in You!

PSALM 89:11–14; DEUTERONOMY 32:4; JEREMIAH 29:11

And how grateful I am that You are eternal, and You look beyond today as You allow things in our lives that help us become our best, both for our future here on earth and for eternity. I praise You that even Satan's attacks and his efforts to sidetrack us come by Your permission, to help accomplish in and for us the very things he hates.

PSALM 90:2; 1 TIMOTHY 1:17; PSALM 66:10

Thank You that the good name of Your Son, Jesus, is far above all other names—that behind it is the boundless power of His Cross and Resurrection and Ascension. I rejoice that Satan trembles before this matchless name. The war has been won and we're simply bringing in the spoils!

EPHESIANS 1:19–21

So I praise You for the great privilege of knowing You and walking with You and experiencing Your presence with me and in me. Place in my heart a deeper desire to know You better, to live in constant fellowship with You, and to walk worthy of my calling. When I get diverted or distracted or indifferent, cause me to quickly return to a simple trust and delight in You. Make me quickly aware when a spiritual enemy—whether Satan's forces or my flesh or the world—draws me away from You and Your sufficiency. I count on You to bind Satan when he seeks to hinder Your gracious purposes for my life.

EPHESIANS 4:1; COLOSSIANS 1:9–10

I pray You'll do these same things in the lives of Your servants, especially:

_____

_____

_____

_____

_____

DAY 5

EXALTED LAMB, DEFEATED FOE

How I rejoice, Father, that You have seated the Man, Christ Jesus, in the position of highest power at Your right hand. How grateful I am for the agony that You and He went through to make this possible. You let Your beloved Son leave heaven's glory to be born in a stable, cradled in a feeding trough, entrusted to a poor couple from a despised city. Then You let Him suffer on the cross, despised and rejected, bearing all the sin and sorrows of all the ages. How I rejoice that by dying He broke the power of the devil, including the power of death, so that He could liberate us from slavery to sin and from the fear of dying. Then You sealed Your Son's triumph by raising Him from the dead (death could not keep its prey!) and lifting Him to His exalted place far above all other powers, putting all things in subjection under His feet.

ISAIAH 53:2–6; HEBREWS 2:14–15; EPHESIANS 1:20–22

So I worship Your Son, the Lamb who shed His blood for all my sin, the Lamb exalted at Your right hand. How worthy He is of my praise! "Your right hand, O LORD, has become glorious in power; Your right hand, O LORD, has dashed the enemy in pieces."

REVELATION 5:12; EXODUS 15:6 (NKJV)

I praise You that the day will come when Jesus will abolish all rule and authority and power, and with our eyes we'll actually see all enemies put under His feet. Then He'll deliver the kingdom up to You, Father, that You may be all in all.

1 CORINTHIANS 15:24–28

I rejoice that because our Lord Jesus disarmed the devil and canceled his authority, our enemy is now a wounded beast headed for eternal punishment. He is a defeated foe, along with all his army of demons! How glad I am that You've pronounced the judicial verdict against them, though their final defeat has not yet been carried out. In Your great wisdom and long-range purposes, You allow the enemy a degree of freedom to deceive and attack human beings on the earth—but only until his final and eternal punishment in the lake of fire. Even now it's only under Your sovereign power and wisdom that he's able to prowl the earth.

COLOSSIANS 2:15; REVELATION 20:2, 10

I'm so grateful that You, my all-powerful God, are in supreme control and that You protect me as I put my faith in Your Son's triumph over all the forces of evil. Thank You that I can count on You to give continuing and overwhelming victory through our Lord Jesus Christ.

ROMANS 8:37; 1 CORINTHIANS 15:57

THAT DAY!

Father, I rejoice at the day when all evil and all evil powers will be destroyed. "Let the heavens be glad, and let the earth rejoice; let the sea roar, and all it contains; let the field exult, and all that is in it. Then all the trees of the forest will sing for joy before the LORD, for He is coming, for He is coming to judge the earth."

PSALM 96:11–13

At the time of Satan's rebellion, You could have spoken the word and utterly destroyed both him and his fallen angels. Or You could have banished him forever after the fall of Adam and Eve. Instead You've allowed him broad influence and control. Who, Lord, can fully understand Your wisdom, which is so complex, so many-sided?

ROMANS 11:33

I praise You that though at times You may grant the devil power over my circumstances and even over my body, he has no power over my present and eternal relationship with You. And how wonderful to be on

Your side—on the winning side! I rejoice that the day will come when every knee shall bow to Christ and every tongue will confess that He is Lord, to Your glory as God the Father. I worship You because Your grace has been revealed, bringing salvation to all people, and so we can look forward to that wonderful event when the glory of our great God and Savior, Jesus Christ, will be revealed.

PHILIPPIANS 2:10–11; TITUS 2:11–13

I come to sit at Your feet, to listen with my heart as I read Your Word. I come to pour out my love, to worship and bow down. I kneel before You, my Maker, for You are my God and I am a sheep of Your pasture. How grateful I am that I'm Yours! Splendor and majesty, strength and beauty are in Your sanctuary, and I have the privilege of dwelling there! My innermost being is Your holy place—a place of majestic holiness and moral beauty, a place that's eternally undefiled.

PSALM 95:6–7; 100:3; 96:6

I honor Your name; I pray that Your will may be done this day in my life and in my sphere of influence. Fill my heart with the confident hope of Your coming kingdom, and keep me focused on advancing that glorious kingdom today.

MATTHEW 6:10

I pray that Satan will be defeated in all he wants
to do in the following situations:

_____

_____

_____

_____

_____

_____

D A Y
7

SAFE FROM
ACCUSATION

I praise You, my glorious and exalted God,
that when Your Son rose from the grave and
ascended into heaven, You raised *me* with Him! I'm
now seated with Christ in the heavenly realms! He
shares with me His position at Your right hand—a
position of supreme power and victory and
unbelievably close fellowship with You.

EPHESIANS 2:6

This is my privilege, Father, as a citizen of
heaven—part of the birthright that became mine on
that wonderful day I became a member of Your
family. All this was part of Your eternal plan for all
who trust Your Son as their Savior and Master. You
determined these blessings for us even before You
founded the earth. Thank You that I can be
confident of my exalted position and enjoy it
increasingly as I count on these truths.

PHILIPPIANS 3:20; EPHESIANS 1:3–5

So now I'm Your servant, Lord, committed to live for Your glory. I ask You to live out Your life in me with Your love and limitless power. Give me the grace and strength to more and more constantly let You be the answer to my every need...my every shortcoming...my every opportunity to glorify You. Work in me both to will and to do what pleases You.

PSALM 116:16; 86:16; PHILIPPIANS 2:13

I want to give You abundant thanksgiving and praise that I'm Your chosen one, and therefore the enemy cannot succeed in accusing me before You. He may try to bring a charge against me for my sins, but he will fail, for they've all been forgiven—past, present, and future. "Who is in a position to condemn? Only Christ, and Christ died for me, Christ rose for me, Christ reigns in power for me, Christ prays for me."

ROMANS 8:33–34 (PHILLIPS, PERSONALIZED)

Now, Lord, though Satan loves to condemn me and bring charges against me, I need never grovel in the dust with chains around my neck. How I praise You for this! You have broken those chains! You have cleansed me and given me new garments of righteousness and praise instead of despair. So day by day I can rise up, put on those beautiful garments, and worship You in holy array—in the beauty of holiness.

ISAIAH 61:3, 10; 52:1–2; PSALM 29:2

How grateful I am, Father, for how these truths are mine to believe and meditate on. I thank You for the way they help me maintain my victory over Satan and his evil powers. May this victory become more full and constant in my life—and in my fellow believers, especially:

_____

_____

_____

_____

_____

SHAKE OFF THE DUST

Victory—what a word, Lord! A word full of meaning: overwhelming triumph, eternal and complete. And how grateful I am that Christ's victory is mine—part of the position and privileges that You gave me when I became Yours.

I praise You that no demons—no ruling spirits of any kind—now have any authority over me. How amazing and glorious that all my spiritual enemies have been judged and exposed as losers, eternally defeated losers. I no longer need to fear them, though I still need to resist them as I draw near to You day by day, hour by hour.

ROMANS 8:37–39; COLOSSIANS 2:15

Because You've prepared me in Christ for victories over the enemy, I shake off the dust and rise up. I loose myself from any bondage of the flesh or of Satan, and I put on the Lord Jesus Christ, clothing myself with Him as my strength.

ISAIAH 52:1–2; ROMANS 13:14

Thank You, Lord, that Your name—Your wonderful, all-powerful name!—is a strong tower where I can be safe and encouraged. You are my Rock, my Refuge, and my Rescuer. You give me a way to escape from the attacks of all my spiritual enemies, from the unseen spiritual rulers and authorities of this world's darkness. Thank You for giving me in Christ a place of safety and protection. As one of Your loved ones I can rest in Your arms; I can lie down in safety, close to You, assured that You protect me all night long as well as all day long. What promises and privileges are mine!

PROVERBS 18:10; PSALM 71:3; DEUTERONOMY 33:12 (NCV)

You are my strength every morning, my salvation in times of distress. You're the stability of my times. So I clothe myself with my beautiful garment of praise. I treasure the safety You've provided from any crafty attacks by the enemy—from anything that would not be for my ultimate good or for the advance of the Good News. Even when You allow severe trials in my life, You know my path; and when You have tried me, I shall come forth as gold.

ISAIAH 33:2; 61:3; ROMANS 8:28; PHILIPPIANS 1:12; JOB 23:10

I pray that in new ways and with greater constancy my life will be victorious. May I be a glory to

Your name hour by hour, defeating Satan's purposes regardless of what happens. And I pray the same for all Your children and servants—especially:

_____

_____

_____

_____

_____

_____

_____

VICTORY AS
WE TESTIFY

I glorify You, Father, for You are exalted on high, far above all evil powers, and You've given me victory over the devil who accuses Your people day and night. What a privilege that I can pray with confidence and stand firmly against the ways the enemy tries to accuse or condemn or discredit me.

REVELATION 12:10

You are my Strength and Glory; through You I can repel the onslaught of the enemy. I praise You that the keys to victory are mine as I let You be the Lord of my life—as by simple faith I depend on the death and resurrected life of Your Son. How I thank You that His tremendous power is available to me!

ISAIAH 28:5–6; EPHESIANS 1:19 (PHILLIPS)

Thank You too for the critical blow that came to Satan when Jesus shed His blood for my sins, dying in my place to pay the penalty I deserved— then rising from the dead, ascending to glory, and

coming to live in and through each believer. You
clothe me with strength so I can resist my enemies—
the world with its lust and pride, the flesh, and the
devil with his temptations and accusations.

JOHN 12:31; 16:11; 1 JOHN 2:16

I praise You for how Your Spirit fills us with
power and courage to speak the truth of the gospel.
Thank You that He convicts people of sin, convinces
them of truth through the crucified and risen Christ,
and releases them from the power of Satan to You.
How I rejoice that the evil ruler of this world has been
judged!

ACTS 26:18; JOHN 16:8–11

I'm so grateful for the victories that come as we
testify to believers as well as unbelievers, proclaiming the
Good News of our Savior's death and resurrection and
kingly control. How I rejoice that our testimony and
sharing of Your Word defeats Satan in the lives of
people, both those he has blinded spiritually and
believers he's seeking to ensnare.

ACTS 1:8; 2 CORINTHIANS 4:4

I gladly welcome the powerful, invisible
weapons You've made available for us. I praise You
that they have divine power to demolish strongholds

and to take captive every thought, making it
obedient to Christ—and that this includes my
thoughts! Enable me to use these weapons wisely
and continuously.

2 CORINTHIANS 10:4-5

And I give You thanks, as the mighty Deliverer,
for the way praise works to expel the power of the evil
one. Give me the grace to continue in praise and
prayer until Satan is defeated in the following lives and
situations:

_____

_____

_____

_____

_____

_____

MY PART IN THE BATTLE FOR OTHERS

Thank You, Lord, for the part I can have in Your spiritual battle to rescue people from Satan's dark kingdom and prepare them to reign with You forever. I praise You, Lord, for the challenging plan You have for me to invest my life in. Thank You that this plan includes walking close to You, helping others know and enjoy this same closeness, and using my spiritual gift.

ACTS 26:18; COLOSSIANS 3:16–17; 1.CORINTHIANS 7:7

I rejoice that You are mightily at work against the enemy's purposes as he cleverly seeks to blind and destroy both believers and unbelievers. Empower me to do my part in this work and to endure opposition and hardship as Your soldier. Help me constantly rejoice that I'm on the winning side.

2 TIMOTHY 2:3, 10

You have shown us that the prince of the power of the air is actively at work in those who don't know

and obey You—to blind them, to entice them to evil,
and to use them against Your purposes and against
Your servants. But You've promised that in You—in
the power of Your might—we are strong and we can
call on You to release Your mighty power. You are our
refuge and strength, a very present help in trouble—
abundantly available to help in tight places. Thank You
that this is true not only for us but for all who will
come to faith in You and grow spiritually because of
our testimony.

EPHESIANS 2:2; 6:10; COLOSSIANS 1:11; PSALM 46:1

Make me sensitive to people's needs. Grant me
timely words for those who are weary, and special
grace to share with them the reason for the wonderful
hope I have.

ISAIAH 50:4; 1 PETER 3:15

With all the tensions and complaints and disputes
in this world, even among Your people, thank You for
asking me to be a peacemaker. Use me, Lord, to help
heal broken hearts and broken relationships that divide
families and churches and communities. All this division
is not from You, Lord; it's from the devil himself, who
loves to see Christians arguing and fighting and
disunited. I worship You as the only one who can help
Your people change this.

PHILIPPIANS 2:14; JAMES 3:18

I call on You, Lord, to work deeply in those who
need greater unity—groups that I'm in touch with,
such as:

_____

_____

_____

_____

_____

Also people and families I'm concerned about,
such as:

_____

_____

_____

_____

_____

Do something special through Your Word and Your
Spirit to heal wounds and unite hearts. How I praise
You that Jesus is Victor over Satan and his
divisiveness.

DAY 11

STRONG IN YOUR ROYAL FAMILY

Thank You that You are the great, faithful God who longs to give each of Your children personal daily victories over the evil one, as well as long-term victories. "O my soul, march on with strength."

JUDGES 5:21

Thank You for the inner strength that comes from knowing I can call You "Father, dear Father." And how amazing it is that Your Son is not ashamed to call us brothers and sisters. I rejoice that You—the awesome Creator of the universe and all things in it, including all people—have given us the privilege of actually being Your children, born of You, and included as members of Your royal family for all eternity!

GALATIANS 4:6 (PHILLIPS); HEBREWS 2:11; 1 JOHN 3:1

I praise You that these privileges give me increasing strength and victory through our Lord Jesus Christ—victory over Satan and all his schemes, victory over the world system and all its corruption, and victory over my own fleshly nature and failings. What a privilege, what a joy divine to be able to lean with full confidence on Your everlasting arms, which enable me to thrust out the enemy.

1 CORINTHIANS 15:57; DEUTERONOMY 33:27

You are well able, Lord, to defeat my spiritual enemies, even as You defeated Israel's enemies in Old Testament times. In the name of Jesus I count on You to demoralize these enemies. Confuse them, confound their strategies, and cause them to panic. Bring their plans to nothing.

ISAIAH 19:2-3

Let all Your enemies perish, O Lord; but let everyone who loves You "be like the rising of the sun in its might." Thank You that Christ has delivered me from the realm of Satan, the prince of darkness, and has brought me into the light of Your marvelous love—into the light of knowing Your glory. I rejoice that I no longer need to walk in darkness, for I have the light of life.

JUDGES 5:31; 2 CORINTHIANS 4:6

Father, may I and my fellow believers absorb Your light more fully and depend on Your strength more constantly. More and more may we triumph in Christ and spread abroad the wonderful fragrance of Your indwelling presence.

2 CORINTHIANS 2:14

Especially defeat Satan in the lives of Your children struggling with various temptations—including the following friends and loved ones:

_____

_____

_____

_____

_____

ANOINTED WITH POWER

Father, I praise You that Christ, anointed with Your Holy Spirit and power, continues to conquer new territory within me, filling me afresh with Your fullness, Your love, Your power.

ACTS 10:38

Thank You that Christ is my risen and victorious Lord, and that in Him I've been anointed with Your Spirit to reign in life—to triumph over sin and over the evil one with his lies and deceptions. How wonderful to know, Father, that right now Your Spirit intermingles with my spirit in a permanent oneness. I look to Him to continually fill me and to keep me under His influence, so that His gracious and immeasurable power will be at work in me, overcoming my flesh and the world and the devil.

2 CORINTHIANS 1:21–22; 1 JOHN 2:20

I rejoice that Your Spirit is here to convict me of sin, to protect me from Satan, and to strengthen me with might. Thank You that this anointing I've received from

You abides in me and continues to teach me—and His teaching is true, and not a lie. And through His truth I've been set free—free from the mastery of sin and the snares of Satan, free to reign in the realm of Real Life. I rejoice that the truth counters Satan's lies. It cancels out his subtle deceptions.

1 JOHN 2:27; JOHN 8:32

I'm especially grateful to You for giving me power to be effective in serving You. I praise You that I can serve by Your Spirit's power mightily at work within me, rather than having to depend on my own strength and abilities.

ACTS 1:8; COLOSSIANS 1:29

I pray for myself and for the many Christians I know, both individually and in various groups, that we'll be enriched through a growing knowledge of You. And may it dawn on us afresh that You have been made rich because we belong to You—we are Your inheritance! Encourage us through Your Word and the enlightening of Your Spirit. Make us more aware of the tremendous power available to us, to assure victory over all the evil powers we encounter.

EPHESIANS 1:17–19

And Father, I praise You that this close relationship with You can also knit me together with other believers by strong ties of love. I realize that loving, harmonious unity with other believers is always one of the great needs in our lives as Your children, and we can count on You to accomplish it. I praise You for the great protection this provides against the attacks and deceptions of our enemy.

May I—and those I pray for—increasingly understand and *experience* the rich fullness and oneness that is ours in Christ.

COLOSSIANS 2:1–2

Lord, in my heart I can sing a song of triumph, for victory over the enemy comes not by might nor by power but by Your Spirit. In myself I'm no match for Satan and his demons. But because of Jesus, our Victor, they face impossible odds. They face the One who made the stars and keeps them in their courses—the magnificent One who humbled Himself to die in agony and shame on the cross. What a joy it is to know that through death He broke the power of Satan, our proud and arrogant enemy. And to think that I share His power, that in Him I too can be invincible!

ZECHARIAH 4:6

Thank You that Christ's death and resurrection paved the way for Your Spirit of power to indwell my spirit. Your Spirit has poured out Your love in my heart. He has become in me a spring of water welling up into everlasting life and flowing out as rivers of living water.

ROMANS 5:5; JOHN 4:14; 7:37-39

How deeply grateful I am that by Your Spirit I'm alive with Christ's life and righteous with His righteousness! He is my sufficiency for doing the good works You've planned for me. Thank You for the way this removes the strain from my life—for the way it frees me from the stress of striving in my own strength to please You. It lets me enjoy the calm dews of Your presence with me and in me.

2 CORINTHIANS 3:5–6; EPHESIANS 2:10; HOSEA 14:5

How thankful I am for times of refreshing that come from Your presence. Time and again I can come before You and be renewed. I can let You breathe new life into my inward person day by day as I feast on the abundance of Your house and drink from the rivers of Your delights.

ACTS 3:19; 2 CORINTHIANS 4:16; PSALM 36:8

Thank You that You accept me by Your grace, Your unmerited favor. Make me quick to recognize and resist Satan's lie that I must earn Your love and favor by serving You. What good news it is that grace has replaced law keeping as the way to gain and enjoy spiritual life—the life of Christ Himself! To think that through my inner union with Him I'm accepted, I'm okay, and I'm in the process of being conformed to His image. All through grace!

ROMANS 7:6; EPHESIANS 1:6; ROMANS 8:29

I will sing to You, Lord, for You have triumphed gloriously! You are my strength and my song. You have put a new song in my mouth, a song of praise. May many hear it and trust in You. I praise You that when we begin to praise, we open the way for You to defeat the enemy. We can conquer because we trust in You!

EXODUS 15:1-2; PSALM 40:3; 2 CHRONICLES 20:22

COMPLETELY NEW

Thank You, Lord Jesus, that You came into the world to demonstrate not only Your love but also Your power. You came to give Your life as a sacrifice so sufficient that it canceled all my sins. I'm so grateful that Your death and resurrection crossed out the whole debt against me in Your Father's account book and He no longer keeps a record of the laws I've broken. How wonderful that You nailed that account book to the cross and closed the account. As far as the east is from the west, so far have You removed my transgressions from me.

COLOSSIANS 2:14; PSALM 103:12

Thank You for stripping the demonic rulers and authorities of their power over us—power to accuse and enslave us. And thank You for exposing them as empty and defeated when You triumphed over them through the Cross and the Resurrection. What deliverance and confidence comes through knowing that Satan is defanged and defeated—that You, crucified and now glorified, have dethroned him, breaking the back of his power as the ruler of this world! Now he desperately attempts to maintain a kingdom for himself and to thwart what You seek to do in people's lives. How grateful I am that all my spiritual battles are against an already-beaten and disarmed enemy! What wonderfully good news for me to believe and use!

COLOSSIANS 2:15; HEBREWS 2:14–15; JOHN 12:31

I praise You that You not only removed forever my guilt and sins, but You sent Your Spirit to make me a completely new person—a new creation—in my inmost being. In Your eyes I've been cleansed and perfected forever. By faith—by simple confidence in Your Word—I can be assured of this and enjoy a clean conscience. Thank You, Lord!

2 CORINTHIANS 5:17; HEBREWS 10:14; 9:14

Thank You also for the privilege of encouraging others to believe this good news. Make me bold in sharing these truths, both with believers and unbelievers. Give me grace to take advantage of every opportunity You give, large or small. Help me sow seeds and pray for people in ways that will help defeat Satan's purposes and open their hearts in the coming weeks or months or years—or perhaps today.

COLOSSIANS 4:5

I count on You, Lord, to cause me to triumph in You and to spread to those around me the fragrance that results from knowing You. Enable me to never be ashamed of You and Your wonderful message of good news. Allow me to help others (both believers and not-yet believers) to respond to Your knock at the door of their hearts, letting You do all the good things You've promised for them, both in this life and the next.

2 CORINTHIANS 2:14; REVELATION 3:20

DAY 15

GOOD AND MIGHTY SHEPHERD

"You prepare a table before me in the presence of my enemies; You have anointed my head with oil." Lord Jesus, You are such a Good Shepherd, such a wise and powerful Leader and Protector! I praise You for the amazing truth that You prepare a spiritual banquet for us and that our spiritual enemies have no power to interfere with our feasting.

PSALM 23:5

You will arise and shepherd Your flock "in the strength of the LORD, in the majesty of the name of the LORD." You, Lord Jesus, are our majestic, kingly Shepherd—great to the ends of the earth. You showed Your greatness in open triumph at the Cross and in the Resurrection. And You show it in invisible triumph now, taking ground from Satan and setting his captives free.

MICAH 5:4; COLOSSIANS 2:15

I know that in this present world our enemy is a liar and a vicious lion looking for someone to devour. And as the father of lies he hates the truth and is constantly propagating false ideas and beliefs. His intentions are always evil. Yet how grateful I am that through You, Lord Jesus, the good purposes of our Father in heaven can prevail in the lives of His children. I rejoice that in You we have everything necessary for life and godliness and victory over the enemy.

1 PETER 5:8; JOHN 8:44; 2 PETER 1:3

Father, I magnify You with thanksgiving for placing in Your Son all the glorious riches of wisdom and knowledge, both divine and human. How grateful I am that all Your fullness lives bodily in Christ, and that we as ordinary, flawed Christians have this fullness in us. What a magnificent Savior and Lord You've given us! So much greater and more powerful than all evil influences—including the world, the flesh in each of us, and the devil with all his helpers.

COLOSSIANS 2:3, 9–10

Thank You also for Your Spirit who is my Comforter and Counselor, my Helper and Teacher and intimate Companion. And I praise You that Your Son is preparing a place for us in our eternal Home, so that where He is, we may be also. And there we'll be forever free from all of Satan's evil intentions and influence!

JOHN 14:16, 26: 1–3

I pray that these truths about You and Your Son and Your Spirit will become more and more real in my life, counteracting Satan's lies and false promises. May the same be true for my friends and loved ones—especially:

_____

_____

_____

_____

_____

THE BEST PREOCCUPATION

Thank You, Father, that I need not get preoccupied with the devil and all his conspiracies, or with all the fearful coalitions of enemy rulers and hosts that he supervises. Enable me instead to be preoccupied with You, my holy God. I honor You as the God of Exodus 15—majestic in holiness, awesome in praiseworthy deeds, the almighty Warrior who shatters the enemy. "The LORD is a warrior; Yahweh is His name."

EXODUS 15:11, 3

As I think about the intense spiritual battle we're all in, I may often need to let You tell me, "Take heed, be quiet, do not fear, and do not let your heart be faint." But I need not delve into the power of dark authorities, trying to measure how dangerous they are or pinpoint their specific identities. Thank You that You have revealed in Your Word what we need to know about them and their evil schemes.

ISAIAH 7:4 (RSV); 2 CORINTHIANS 2:11

How good it is to know that the plans and desires of the enemy will not stand. As we walk with You, all his schemes and proposals against us will be thwarted and turned to our advantage, for You are with us. So I choose not to fear the enemy, but to fear only You, with reverent trust and with hatred of evil. I choose not to be preoccupied with Satan, but with You, my all-powerful and all-prevailing God.

PSALM 46:7; ISAIAH 41:10; 14:24, 27

What a joy it is to remember that You've always been victorious and exalted over all the forces in heaven and earth—natural and supernatural, visible and invisible. I praise You that throughout history You have always been behind the scenes, supervising world events—and supervising the spiritual war against Lucifer and all his evil followers, visible and invisible.

NEHEMIAH 9:6; ISAIAH 2:11–12

So I greatly rejoice that You created all spiritual beings, and You remain supreme over them all, including those who are opposed to You. You are infinitely greater than everything we can see as well as everything we can't see, and this includes all satanic rulers and powers, great and small. Satan is accountable to You, as You've shown us in the case of Job. And how I thank You for the countless heavenly authorities who are on Your side—the holy angels who obey Your slightest desire and who are involved with people here on earth as You see fit.

JOB 1:7-12; 2:6; HEBREWS 1:7, 14

Thank You that I'm never at the mercy of Satan, that I need not let him entice me and trap me in sinful ways. Your Word and Spirit make me more aware of his schemes and maneuvers. And I hold fast to this truth: by faith I can stand against him and his evil purposes, both in my life and in the lives of others. I may seldom know just what he's trying to do, or how, but You know. And through You I can stand firm and come away victorious.

DAY 17

GLORY AND SHADOW

Father, help me not to give Satan any advantage or delight by seeking my own glory in people's eyes. Instead let me constantly give glory to You in new ways. May I keep You at center stage as I speak of Your perfections and let You manifest Your presence through me.

Cause me to dwell day by day in Your shadow. I long to live my whole life there, with You in the bright foreground in every situation, in every opportunity. When You work through me, may the praise be Yours. May You be in the limelight as I give all the glory to You and remain in Your shadow.

PSALM 91:1; 86:12; MATTHEW 5:16

Enable me to glorify You as I pass through each situation in my life—each time of blessing or progress, as well as each river I must cross, each desert I must pass through, each season of flood or drought, of pain or pleasure. May my responses honor You, not me. Deliver me from drawing attention to myself either by moaning and complaining or by subtle boasting and trying to impress. Not to me, O Lord, not to me, but to Your name give glory. This prayer is according to Your will, so I can count on You to answer it!

PSALM 115:1; 1 JOHN 5:14–15

O my awesome God, I worship You for Your glory—glory that excels all others—a radiant outshining that makes all other glories fade and ultimately flicker out in oblivion. Thank You that no one has ever been able to rob You of Your glory or share it with You. I shout for joy that Lucifer lost out when he rebelled against Your rule and aspired to steal Your glory and be like the Most High. How he and his legions cringe at the thought of Your glory! How they resent it when we ascribe to You the honor and glory due Your name and refuse to seek glory for ourselves. How the devil hates it when we enthrone You as Lord of our lives and situations, and when we learn to give You the recognition You rightfully deserve.

ISAIAH 48:11; DANIEL 4:37

I worship You for Your Majesty as the Most High God, exalted far above all. I worship You for Your brilliance that causes people to fall on their faces before You. I praise Your mighty dignity and awesome beauty as King of all. Yours is a splendor not limited to majestic parades but one that rides forth and wins battles. You're the awesome, glorious Champion, the all-powerful Warrior who prevails against Your enemies.

PSALM 86:9; ISAIAH 42:13; PSALM 45:3–4

To You be the glory, both now and forever. Amen!

ROMANS 11:36; JUDE 24–25

OVERCOMING THE WORLD

Thank You, Lord, that Your desire is not to take us out of the world, but to keep us safe from the evil one, making us strong and pure and holy as You teach us Your words of truth.

JOHN 17:15–17

How grateful I am that I've been crucified to the world, which lies in the grip of the evil one, and I can boldly stand against worldly desires to indulge, to possess, to impress. I praise You that though I'm in the world, I'm no longer of the world. Fill me today with a deeper love for You, and make me quickly aware when love for the world creeps in.

1 JOHN 2:16–17; GALATIANS 2:20; 6:14

Thank You again for redeeming me from indwelling sin—from sin in the flesh—from the patterns and energies of my former way of life. I've been born out of the old life into a new life as a new person in Christ. I rejoice that You've united me with Christ—with His crucifixion, His resurrection, His ascension. What a joy to be assured that Christ *is* my

Life—that my life is "hidden with Christ in God"—and that I have the Holy Spirit within me to enlighten, to empower, to be my Ally and Mentor and Guide, and to bring a harvest of godly qualities.

2 Corinthians 5:17; Colossians 3:3–4; Galatians 5:22–23

I look forward to the day when my body will be resurrected and sin in my flesh will be left behind, never again to influence me. Thank You that in my innermost being, in my spirit, this separation has already occurred—and that the cross and the empty tomb stand between my new life and those old patterns and energies.

Romans 6:3–4

I embrace Your promise that by the Spirit I can be free from the down-pull of the flesh. May I throughout this day see myself as You see me; may I count myself dead to sin—separated from it—and alive to You. Make me quickly aware when I let the old ways invade my experience. Enable me by the Holy Spirit to put to death the deeds of the flesh—to make definite, decisive choices against sin and for obedience.

Romans 6:11; 8:13

I praise You that the Holy Spirit is within me to fill me and perform His wonderful ministry in and through me. I yield myself to His loving control and pray that He will produce in me the fruit of the Spirit, to Your glory.

2 Corinthians 7:1; Galatians 5:16

My
Unassailable
Wall

Lord, I praise You that I can rely on You to
protect me—to guard me day and night
from the tactics and power of Satan and his evil
spirits. I thank You that I can be strong and let my
heart take courage, along with all who hope in You.

PSALM 31:24

How I rejoice in Your "lovingkindness"! I thank
You that in any trial I face You see my affliction and
know the troubles of my soul, and You don't give me
over into the hand of the enemy. You set my feet in a
large place, where I can stand firm and not slip and fall.
How good it is to be Your servant and loved one!

PSALM 31:7–8

You are my perfect Refuge, though the worst may
come upon me—distress, grief, slander, even
persecution. I'm so glad You're my Deliverer when
Satan conspires against me, directly or through people,
seeking to destroy me emotionally, spiritually, even
physically. I take my stand against him in Jesus' name. I

trust in You, for You are my God; my times are in Your hand, not in the hand of any enemy, visible or invisible. My destiny is under Your control, not Satan's. I count on You to deliver in both current and future attacks. My eyes are continually toward You, for You will pluck my feet out of the net.

PSALM 31:14–16; 25:15

I praise You for how You're able to turn my enemies back, to drive them away like chaff before the wind, to pursue them and make their way dark and slippery. I don't need to fret because of the enemy and his devices, his snares, his attacks, his hindrances and obstacles. In You I can rest and be still and wait patiently for You to work, without fretting or despairing.

PSALM 35:4–6; PSALM 37:7

Thank You that as I trust You with a steadfast mind, Your presence is around me as a strong, unassailable wall and beneath me as an everlasting Rock. I rejoice that You're like a wall of fire around me to keep the enemy away and to provide me with warmth and light. I count on You to keep that wall of protection around me, a wall that Satan cannot penetrate. May Your mighty presence guard my mind and emotions. My life is precious to You; rescue it from the lions.

ISAIAH 26:1–4; ZECHARIAH 2:5; PSALM 35:17 (NIV)

I pray this also for others near and far who are experiencing the enemy's attacks. I intercede especially for:

_____

_____

_____

_____

_____

_____

MY COMPLETE ARMOR

Thank You, Father, for Your gracious and loving command to be strong in You and in Your mighty power, putting on Your full armor. Give me grace to do this day by day, hour by hour.

EPHESIANS 6:10–11

You tell us that our fight is not against visible enemies but against the invisible forces of evil—the satanic forces which often work through humans, moving them to resist You and oppose us as Your servants. I affirm with confidence that You are infinitely greater than all these opponents. And I praise You for providing this complete armor so that I can stand firm against my spiritual enemies. I rejoice that I can be assured of victory and protected from every attack the enemy could ever conceive against me.

EPHESIANS 6:12–13

Thank You for each piece of armor—the belt of truth...the breastplate of righteousness...the footwear which the Good News of peace supplies...the shield of faith...the helmet of salvation...and the sword of the Spirit, which is Your Word. How I thank You for these, for they are not luxuries or nice options, but necessities. They prepare me for righteous living as well as for success in battle. Teach me to wear my armor constantly.

EPHESIANS 6:14–17

I thank and praise You for the tremendous realities these pieces of armor represent. They're a part of "every spiritual blessing in the heavenlies" which You've lavished on me in Christ. And they're a vital part of Your plan for delivering me from the corrupt and destructive behaviors and thoughts that Satan promotes.

EPHESIANS 1:3 (BERKELEY MARGIN)

I praise You that You Yourself are my protective armor, both within me and around me. You're the defense of my life and I can leave everything quietly to You. "Rock, rescue, refuge, You are all to me. Never shall I be overthrown.... My safety and my honor rest on You."

PSALM 27:1; 62:1–2, 7 (MOFFATT, PERSONALIZED)

I thank You, Father, that putting on my armor is so closely linked with putting on the Lord Jesus Christ, for He is the Truth; He is our Righteousness and our

Peace; He is the Author of our faith and our salvation; and He is the Word of God. I rejoice that wearing the armor means knowing and experiencing Him in ways that uniquely prepare us for protection and victory.

JOHN 14:6; 1 CORINTHIANS 1:30; EPHESIANS 2:14;
HEBREWS 12:2; 2:10; REVELATION 19:13

I count on these truths, Lord, as I face the needs and responsibilities of today and the coming days. Bring blessings out of the needs and problems that Satan would like to use as hindrances. And may the same be true for:

_____

_____

_____

_____

_____

_____

BELT OF TRUTH

Thank You, Lord, for the strong belt of truth
You ask me to put on as my first piece of
armor. How I rejoice in Your revealed truth which is
so powerful, so vital. It serves like a soldier's belt did
in ancient times, holding up his flowing garments,
letting him move fully and freely without tripping.
May the truths of Your Word do the same for me! I
rejoice that I can count on You to bring to mind the
truth I need in each temptation that comes my way,
in each spiritual battle I face.

EPHESIANS 6:14

Thank You for letting me know that Satan is the
father of lies and has been a liar from the beginning.
I'm so grateful that You have lifted me out of the
quicksand of his lies about who You are, about who I
am, and about what life is meant to be. Thank You
especially for exposing his lies about Your goodness—
about Your positive plans and intentions for me, Your
plans for my well-being and my highest good. He wants

me to believe that You hem me in and hold me back from really living. He wants to lure me into something that looks like Your plan, but with subtle and deadly differences. Thank You for how You repeatedly sweep away his lies, big or small, in which I'm tempted to seek refuge or fulfillment.

JEREMIAH 29:11

I worship You as the God of truth—good, solid truth. I rejoice that You see and reveal things as they truly are. Your whole Being is reality. Falseness or falsehood can make no inroads into You. You have no blind spots, no decay through deceit of any kind. All Your words are reliable, never deceiving, never leading astray, never leading to false confidence. You're always faithful, always true to Your promises. You are the Light of my life, and in You there is no darkness at all. So I have no fear of being deceived or defrauded by You, no fear of being let down or forsaken.

DEUTERONOMY 7:9; REVELATION 19:11;
2 TIMOTHY 2:13; 1 JOHN 1:5

I praise You that through Your Word You give me wisdom and understanding, so that I can experience reality and see things from Your point of view. Thank You, Lord, that as the God of truth, You have ransomed me. And now Your truth keeps me from basing my life on feelings or fantasies. In Your light, I see light.

COLOSSIANS 1:9; PSALM 31:5; 36:9

I ask You to implant Your truth in my heart in new ways as I read and study and memorize the Scriptures. Grip my heart day by day with the insights I especially need. As I meditate on Your words, may they deeply penetrate my heart and life, so that I will not be tripped up or led astray by the world or the flesh or the devil.

BREASTPLATE OF RIGHTEOUSNESS

Thank You, Lord, for calling us to "lay aside the deeds of darkness and put on the armor of light." I'm so glad that our armor isn't some stiff metal covering, but something as beautiful and bright and weightless and flexible as light itself!

ROMANS 13:12

Thank You especially for the shining breastplate of righteousness which You gave me as I came to trust You as my Savior. What a protection this is for my heart! How grateful I am that You have given me Your righteousness in exchange for my sin—that Your Son, Jesus, actually bore all my sin on the cross, becoming sin for me—and that now I'm righteous in my innermost being. I'm so glad You've made me eternally holy and clean in Your sight, always able to come boldly to Your throne of grace with utter confidence.

EPHESIANS 6:14; 2 CORINTHIANS 5:21; HEBREWS 4:16

I praise You that knowing and believing this helps me live in a way that pleases You, preventing

Satan from getting a foothold in my life. I rejoice that in You I have the power to renounce evil and cultivate righteous living. I count on You to lead me today in the paths of righteousness.

Psalm 23:3

I rejoice that the righteousness You've given me is the very righteousness of Christ. What a losing battle it would be if I had to depend on my own righteousness—on self-righteousness, which is like filthy rags in Your sight.

1 Corinthians 1:30; Philippians 3:9; Isaiah 64:6

I praise You for being a righteous God. You love righteousness and hate wickedness. You never have ulterior motives. You're utterly reliable and You're always good, never evil. My righteous God, I worship You in the Spirit, I glory in Christ Jesus, and I choose to put no confidence in the flesh—in any works of righteousness I myself might be able to produce. I know I have no actual righteousness of my own in Your sight—and I refuse to try to establish any. Instead, I rest completely in the righteousness that's mine through Your Son—inner righteousness that leads to righteous living. And thank You for the results of righteousness: peace and quietness, confidence and gladness now and forever.

Hebrews 1:9; Philippians 3:3; Isaiah 32:17

I'm so grateful for Christ's example in wearing the breastplate: "In righteousness He judges and wages war." What a victory word *righteousness* is! What a power word! "The righteousness of the upright will deliver them." By faith I accept the liberating truth that my true self is strong and righteous through the work of Christ on the cross and through my union with Him. Therefore I can triumph when the enemy accuses and attacks.

REVELATION 19:11; PROVERBS 11:6

READY WITH THE GOSPEL OF PEACE

Thank You, Lord, that we can equip our feet with readiness to proclaim the gospel of peace as part of our armor for staying strong in You. How glad I am that it includes a threefold victory over sin—over its penalty, its power, and eventually over its presence. Thank You for how simple the gospel message is—that Christ died for our sins and was buried, and rose again the third day. And thank You for the privilege of sharing this good news simply, with Your Spirit's power and love and sensitivity.

EPHESIANS 6:15; 3:8 (NLT)

How I treasure this good news of Christ's victory over sin and Satan—this glad message that tunes us in to the unsearchable riches—the endless treasures—available in Christ. And how grateful I am for the way the gospel protects my feet from wounds that would cause me to fall in battle. Thank You that it sets my heart free to run in the path of

Your commands—it turns me from Satan's control to Your gracious rule over me.

PSALM 119:32 (NIV)

I marvel at how this good news has drawn me into Your kingdom and given me peace with You both now and for all eternity. I'm no longer Your enemy! I belong to You, along with all who have heard the gospel and responded with simple faith.

ROMANS 10:17; 1 CORINTHIANS 1:18

What a joy it is to be at peace with You—to be permanently linked with You, with all the enmity ended, the alienation gone forever. Thank You that this "shalom" peace includes wholeness, contentment, harmony, and well-being. What inner rest this provides—freedom from the turmoil and anxieties that would drain my strength for battle.

ROMANS 5:1

But, Lord, how Satan loves to divert us from the gospel of peace and prod us to fight the wrong battles—fleshly battles with one another as we step into Your shoes to judge others. The flesh prods us to side with Satan as the accuser, directing our anger at people. Deliver us from this temptation!

ROMANS 14:4

Lord Jesus, You are our deep inner peace even in the midst of battle—a victorious peace won by the cosmic battle You fought in Gethsemane, on the

Cross, and in the Resurrection. And because You shepherd us, we can live in spiritual safety as we let You work in us. Your presence within us speaks, "Peace, be still," giving a calm sense of protection from the enemy.

JOHN 16:33; COLOSSIANS 1:20; JOHN 14:27

Today I pray for this peace in the lives of Your children—and especially for:

_____

_____

_____

_____

_____

_____

SHIELD OF FAITH

How glad I am, Lord, that the complete armor You've given us includes the shield of faith—a massive shield that prevents damage from the flaming arrows Satan uses to attack our faith and our walk with You.

EPHESIANS 6:16

Thank You, Lord, that faith comes through feeding on—and counting on—Your Word. And thank You that the shield of faith includes believing everything You've said about Yourself and Your Son and Your Spirit. Thank You for Your grace in which I stand and for all You have provided for me. I count on my position in Christ far above the enemy and on the indwelling Holy Spirit who has sealed me and who fills me for obedience and service. I rejoice that I don't have to fight my way to a position of safety. Instead, by simple faith, I choose to resist the enemy from a platform of safety—safety based on the victory You have already provided. I can reign in life through

Christ. I can be strong and stand firm in the faith.

ROMANS 10:17; 5:2; EPHESIANS 2:6; 1:13; 5:18;
ROMANS 5:17; 1 CORINTHIANS 16:13

I praise You that I can fix my eyes on Jesus, the Author and Finisher of my faith. I can count on Him as my ever-present Commander and Friend who gives me strength and victory. I choose an attitude of faith and confidence as I face the enemy in the name and merits of the highest Authority in heaven and on earth—in the name of Jesus, Your Son, the almighty Victor.

HEBREWS 12:2

Father, I choose to put on the Lord Jesus Christ as my strength and my shield—my inner and outer protection. In whatever ways Satan desires to defeat me in today's battle, I pray in Jesus' name that You will not let his evil devices succeed. Nullify the enemy's counsel. Thwart him, upset him, and frustrate his plans. Do not let my enemy exult over me!

ROMANS 13:14; PSALM 25:2

Thank You for Your promise that You will be with me, and that You will hide me in the secret shelter of Your presence. So by faith I choose today to dwell in You—to trust in Your all-protective presence which evil powers cannot pierce. You may let distressing things happen to me, but I count on You to protect me from

Satan's purposes. Build a wall around my life, a strong
defense grounded on truth after truth which I choose to
believe. I thank You that I can live by simple faith, by
simple confidence in You and Your all-embracing
salvation, past, present, and future. Work deeply in me
so that I'll constantly count on the promises You've
given, looking to You to work in me, for me, and
through me.

EXODUS 33:14; PSALM 31:20; 140:13; 56:3

Enable me to use my shield of faith day by day
and hour by hour. And do the same for my fellow
soldiers—especially:

_____

_____

_____

_____

_____

HELMET OF SALVATION

Thank You, gracious God, for the helmet of salvation—salvation by Jesus' death from the penalty of sin, and salvation by His life in me from the power of sin—from the indwelling fleshly tendencies that can give Satan inroads into my life. "O God the LORD, the strength of my salvation, You have covered my head in the day of battle."

EPHESIANS 6:17; PSALM 140:7

I rejoice that the helmet of salvation protects my thinking and helps assure that You are delivering me from sin and from the snares and attacks of Satan. I realize this doesn't guarantee a trouble-free life, but I thank You that it does guarantee a joyful and purposeful life, no matter what Satan has in mind.

How crafty our enemy is as he seeks to lead me astray from sincere and pure devotion to You! How deeply he wants to wound and control me. And how easy it is to let the world squeeze me into its mold, into its ways of thinking. Enable me to fully commit my mind to You in all that I think and in all that I expose it to. Give me grace to be careful what I listen to and think about, knowing that my life is shaped by my thoughts. And may I not think of myself more highly than I ought to. May I make no provision for the flesh in my thought life, to satisfy its cravings.

2 CORINTHIANS 11:3; ROMANS 12:3; 13:14

I'm so grateful I can count on You to work in me afresh day by day and hour by hour, saving me from all sin. May my thinking and my loyalties and my plans be centered in You and Your Word. May I let You show me how to use my time, where to focus my attention, and how to handle my emotions. Thank You for the way this frees You to do so many of the things I pray for. It lets You remold my mind from within, so I can experience Your good and totally perfect will. It opens the way for me to become more fully pleasing to You. And it helps me resist Satan's determined attempts to manipulate my thinking and words and actions so they fit into his plans. Save me, Lord, from his influence!

ROMANS 12:2

Thank You for inviting me to live more and more in Your presence, where I refuse to dwell on sin in my mind or set any evil thing before my eyes. Help me, Lord, to fix my mind more constantly on Your Word and on Your incomparable love and beauty and perfections. May my mind and heart be filled with delight in You as the High King of heaven, awesome in holiness, mighty to save. Throughout each day, enable me to fix my mind on things that are true and pure— on things that are lovely and kind and gracious.

PSALM 101:3; COLOSSIANS 3:1-2

I pray that You'll enable me to wear my helmet day by day, enjoying Your protection of my mind and my thoughts. And do the same for my fellow soldiers—especially:

_____

_____

_____

_____

_____

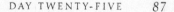

DAY 26

SWORD OF THE SPIRIT

How gracious a provision You've made, Lord, by giving us the sword of the Holy Spirit—Your written Word which is our weapon for both offense and defense. I rejoice at how it attacks the enemy and thwarts his purposes.

EPHESIANS 6:17

Thank You that Your Word pierces like fire and crushes like a sledgehammer. I praise You that Your Word is living and active and sharper than any two-edged sword. It repels Satan and his evil forces, not only in my temptations but also in my praying and my service. Thank You for using Your Word to give special insights in the midst of battle, insights that advance Your purposes and defeat Satan's schemes. Recalling Your Word injects truth into my mind. It delivers me when Satan tries to distort my thinking and mislead me in how I live and how I relate to You and to people. How I love Your Word!

JEREMIAH 23:29; HEBREWS 4:12; PSALM 119:97

How thankful I am for the example Jesus gave us when, at each point of attack, He quoted from the Old Testament to defeat Satan's temptings. With joy I recognize that I, too, can quote Your Word aloud, affirming my faith and rebuking evil powers. I rejoice that my victories when I'm tempted don't depend on my resolutions and good intentions, but on Your specific utterances thrust at the enemy in the power of the Holy Spirit, with an unashamed "It is written."

MATTHEW 4:4, 7, 10

Make me quickly aware when our malicious enemy attacks me by feeding lies into my mind—when he tries to make me question Your goodness or see my present trial or failure as the whole of reality, rather than just one snapshot. Give me grace not to let him sap my strength by going along with his lies and evil intentions. Lead me to fresh Scriptures—or to familiar ones—that counter Satan's lies and refocus my heart on Your point of view.

2 CORINTHIANS 2:11

I rejoice that You and Your Word are Truth, and that Your truth is powerful when I'm tempted or discouraged or confused, and when I fellowship with people or minister to them. What an abundant supply

of wisdom and strength I have as I simply believe
what You've written and come near to You in prayer
and praise! Thank You that Your Word is truth, and
that You use it to make my life more holy and more
useful to You.

PSALM 119:160; JOHN 17:17

I'm so grateful that Your Word has answers to
each need and responsibility that concerns me. Help
me discover these answers—and to hide them in my
heart as Jesus did. And I pray the same for others I
know who are facing temptations or trials:

_____

_____

_____

_____

_____

_____

SPEAKING WITH POWER

Thank You, Lord, for how You continue in our day to speak with power through Your Word, the sword of the Spirit. You've promised that Your Word will not return to You useless. You send forth Your command over the earth and Your Word runs swiftly, controlling the forces of nature, defeating the power and schemes of the adversary. Deliver me from letting my experience of Your written-down truth get stale through neglect. Thank You that Your Word is the Bread of Life which nourishes my soul as I feed on it richly and hide it in my heart—as I let it grip me in a powerful way, just as You intend. May Your Word day by day be the joy and rejoicing of my heart!

ISAIAH 55:11; PSALM 147:15; 119:11; LUKE 4:4; JEREMIAH 15:16

I'm grateful for how You use Your Word to speak through us to others, piercing through to people's needs, convicting them of sin and turning them from darkness to light, from the power of Satan to You. Thank You that the demons tremble when we speak Your Word, as it exposes their lies and shatters their power.

ACTS 26:18; JAMES 2:19

I love Your Word especially because it so vividly displays the wonders of who You are: Your heart of love; Your thoughts and values; Your character with its deep concern for me and all people; Your delight in each of Your children; and Your infinite, boundless power to bless Your loved ones and to defeat the purposes of Satan. How grateful I am for this written revelation of who You are and of how I can be a joy to You, fulfilling Your purposes for my life. Your Word reveals what You want for me and from me. It shows how infinitely greater Your power is than our adversary's, as well as how infinitely better Your purposes are than his. How I praise You for this wonderful Book!

PSALM 119:27

I thank You again that Your Word is a sword that cuts through Satan's power and purposes, enabling me to experience You in all I am and in all I do. Use Your Word in my life day by day. Strengthen me through it and tune me in to Your wisdom. Enhance my delight in it and deepen my knowledge of You...increase my trust in You...and enrich my experience of You as I face the needs and demands of daily life. More and more may Your Word be "the joy and rejoicing of my heart, for I am called by Your name, O LORD God of hosts."

EPHESIANS 6:17; PSALM 1:2; JEREMIAH 15:16 (NKV)

And I pray that You'll do those same things for my loved ones:

_____

_____

_____

_____

_____

_____

PATTERNS OF
PROTECTION

Thank You, almighty God, for the great pattern for protection You've given me in Jesus' prayer in John 17. I pray as He prayed then— that You, dear Father, would preserve and guard me from the evil one, keeping me safe from Satan's power...that I would live as Your sent one in the world...that I would absorb Your joy more constantly and more fully...that I would be made pure and holy by the truth of Your Word...that I would live in loving unity with other believers...and that I would experience anew Your love, the same mighty love You have for Jesus!

JOHN 17:13, 15, 17, 19, 23, 26

I praise You that Your Word makes me strong as it lives in me and controls me, and that the Holy Spirit enables me to overcome the evil one as I rely on Him for light and power. I cherish the way Your Spirit makes Your Word alive deep within me in life-changing ways. I rejoice that in every type of circumstance, the truths of Your Word enable me to pray according to Your will and to experience Your answers.

JOHN 15:7; 1 JOHN 2:14; 5:14–15

Thank You for Your warnings not to love the world and its ways. Train me instead to love and serve You the way You want me to. Work in me so that I will continually focus my heart and mind on You and persevere in running the race You've set before me.

1 JOHN 2:15–16; HEBREWS 12:1–2

Give me special grace, Lord, not to become entangled in the affairs of this world, but to be a good soldier in Your army, willing to endure hardships for You. Show me any ways I fall short in this…. Make me alert against the satanic forces that control the world system, as they seek to take me captive through hollow and deceptive ideas. What pressures and temptations come my way from people who don't know You, from many of the world's amusements, and from the enemy who's at work in them! How glad I am that Your Word and Your Spirit protect me from "empty philosophy and high-sounding nonsense that come from human thinking and from the evil powers of this world, and not from Christ."

2 TIMOTHY 2:3–4; COLOSSIANS 2:8 (NLT)

I'm also grateful that You're a Warrior who does not become weary or tired. You energize me and renew my strength as I wait on You. You give strength both for daily living and for battling against our spiritual enemy. How grateful I am that when I'm weary and have no strength and stumble badly, I can let You be my strength and vitality.

Isaiah 40:28–31

I pray for renewed strength and vigor for others I know who may be weary:

_____

_____

_____

_____

_____

_____

WHILE ENEMIES RAGE

You are at work, Lord, reaching down into the cauldron of this fallen world, drawing people to Yourself and conforming them to Your likeness. And one by one You are bringing many sons and daughters to glory. For all this I praise You. This is Your glorious purpose for humanity's history, and You've been at it all these centuries and millennia. How wonderful that You let us have a part in fulfilling it!

2 CORINTHIANS 3:18; HEBREWS 2:10; ROMANS 9:22–24

Thank You for letting us know that Satan is shrewd, that he's wise in a perverted way and has thousands of years of experience. Yet not one of the plans he has masterminded against You and Your family and kingdom has truly succeeded. Our enemy scores many victories in his dark kingdom. He blinds people, plucking away the Word when it is sown. He causes much trouble for believers and for the church, sowing tares, tempting, deceiving—all with Your permission. He may score points in the contest, destroying effectiveness and even taking lives. But he's never able to snatch us out of Your hand.

GENESIS 3:1; 2 CORINTHIANS 2:11; 11:3, 14; JOHN 10:29

Thank You that no wisdom, no understanding, no counsel can prevail against You! While kings and peoples of the earth—part of Satan's dominion—rage against You, You sit in the heavens and scoff at them.

PROVERBS 21:30–31; PSALM 2:1–4

You are supreme above all—totally in command—the Commander in Chief of spiritual armies. How I rejoice that You are the Master of breakthroughs against our spiritual enemies and their evil purposes. Show Yourself strong today, O God; command strength and victory as You act on our behalf.

2 SAMUEL 5:20 (NAS MARGIN); PSALM 68:28

I honor You because You are infinitely greater than the god of this world, who blinds people to keep them in spiritual darkness. You are Light that penetrates into darkened souls, shattering their blindness, opening their eyes. You are Truth that exposes Satan's deceptions and dispels false beliefs and dependencies. You are Spirit that penetrates the spirits of those who believe, giving them eternal life, infusing their innermost being with Your light.

ISAIAH 29:18; 2 CORINTHIANS 4:4–6

I praise You that the ultimate victory of our Lord Jesus will extend to all things everywhere, defeating everything evil, both visible and invisible. All evil beings will be banished forever. And there will be no more darkness, for everything will be illumined by Your powerful light. Hallelujah! For our Lord God Almighty reigns!

REVELATION 21:23–25; 22:3–5; 19:6

DAY
30

THE PATH TO MY DESTINY

Father, before I received Christ I was Your enemy. I was on the wrong side in the war between Satan and You. I was born with a fallen nature, born into the wrong kingdom as part of the opposition. And unwittingly, when I knew enough to choose, I repeatedly chose for sin and against You! Unknowingly I signed on with the rebel prince—the god of this world, the prince of the power of the air.

COLOSSIANS 1:21; ROMANS 5:10

How I praise You again for transferring me from that dark domain into the kingdom of Your beloved Son. Through Him You rescued me from the tyrant's power. You opened my eyes so that the truth about Jesus dawned in my heart, causing me to be born again. Now I'm at peace with You—aligned with You, made one with You as a member of Your very own family and a citizen of Your country. You took me from my lowliness and seated me with princes, destined with Christ to inherit the throne of glory. In this world I'm only a stranger, an alien, an exile, a pilgrim heading for my true Homeland, the glorious city You've prepared.

COLOSSIANS 1:13; EPHESIANS 2:19; 1 SAMUEL 2:8;
HEBREWS 11:13; 13:14; PSALM 113:5–8

How wonderful that my enmity with You has ended—I'm no longer a "child of wrath," imprisoned in Satan's world system that rightly calls forth Your anger and condemnation. I'm no longer united with sin; I'm no longer condemned. You've made me alive with Christ, and able by His power to overcome every trap and attack of our spiritual enemy. So now I'm fighting on Your side in the ages-long spiritual war. What a relief, what a joy to strive *for* You against the enemy rather than strive against You!

EPHESIANS 2:2–6

Yes, You ended my striving against You and my alignment with Your enemies. And at how great a price! You paid for my redemption with the precious blood of Your Son. Once again I gladly praise You for Your abundant love and mercy. Thank You that nothing—even Satan's strongest onslaught—can ever separate me from Your love. "Death can't, and life can't. The angels can't, and the demons can't. My fears for today, my worries about tomorrow, and even the powers of hell can't keep Your love away."

ROMANS 8:38–39 (NLT, PERSONALIZED)

I worship You, and count on You to work in me today both to will and to do what pleases You. And may these truths become more real to the new believers in Your family—especially:

_____

_____

_____

_____

_____

_____

_____

THE LAST WORD

Thank You, Lord, that You always have the last word, not Satan.

How grateful I am for Your ultimate victory over the devil and all his plans. You will deliver us forever from his presence and all his evil influence, and Your victory will be clearly seen in all the earth. In that day You will fully enforce Satan's defeat, binding him and exiling him to eternal torment. Your kingdom will be exalted above all others, and people from around the world will stream to Your headquarters to hear You teach them Your ways. "Great and marvelous are Your works, Lord God Almighty!... All nations shall come and worship before You."

REVELATION 20:10; MICAH 4:1–2; REVELATION 15:3–4 (NKJV)

I praise You that You have promised us eternal victory, with total freedom from the presence of sin— and for letting us begin now to share in that victory. I'm so glad that Your salvation brings freedom not only from the penalty of sin but also from the power of sin in our daily lives. Thank You for granting us deliverance from the cravings of indwelling sin and from following its desires and thoughts.

ROMANS 6:4–7

I eagerly await that day when, by Your personal call to be with You or by Your glorious return, You'll take me to be with You for eternity, along with all believers. Help me focus my heart continually on the wonders of Your return and Your ultimate, total triumph. I praise You that what we'll then see is far beyond our present imaginings. I look forward to feasting my eyes on Your shining glory, with Your eyes bright like flames of fire and Your face like a brilliant noonday sun. How awesome it will be to hear Your voice thundering like the sound of many waters—like mighty ocean waves and a thousand Niagaras. And how delightful it will be to experience Your warm welcome into Your presence forever. Life's trials will seem so small when we see You!

REVELATION 1:12–16

Thank You that when we come fully into Your presence, we'll be like You for eternity, for we'll see You as You really are. I'm so grateful that this is part of the victory You won at the cross and promised us for the future. How this confident assurance motivates me to live a pure life that glorifies You!

1 THESSALONIANS 4:16–17; PHILIPPIANS 3:20–21; 1 JOHN 3:2–3

Behold, You will come quickly, and Your reward will be with You. Even so, come, Lord Jesus!

REVELATION 22:7, 12, 20

More and more may these glorious truths flood my heart with Your strength and power in the midst of life's joys and trials. And I pray the same for:

_____

_____

_____

_____

_____

_____

II

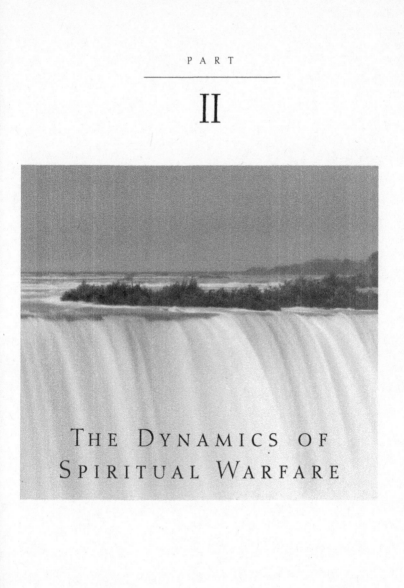

THE DYNAMICS OF
SPIRITUAL WARFARE

ONE

Our Sweeping Victory

We rest on Thee, our Shield and our Defender!
We go not forth alone against the foe;
Strong in Thy strength, safe in Thy keeping tender,
We rest on Thee, and in Thy Name we go.

Behind all spiritual warfare is the intense conflict of Gethsemane and Calvary. There our Lord Jesus was in direct combat with Satan. There He confronted this evil usurper, who fought desperately to keep us in his system of darkness and condemnation—to keep us part of the rebellious system that was under God's wrath.

Satan had long before gained control of the world, bringing darkness, guilt, condemnation, and fear of death. But then God entered the scene, "you might say in disguise," as C. S. Lewis expressed it in *Mere Christianity*; He "landed on this enemy-occupied world in human form." God's own Son slipped right into Satan's territory.

As the prideful Lucifer, Satan had once said, "I will ascend.... I will make myself like the Most High" (Isaiah 14:14). In utter contrast, Jesus "humbled Himself" and "did not regard equality with God a thing to be grasped" (Philippians 2:6–8). He was born to a poor woman of humble social standing, and grew up in obscurity in the despised village of Nazareth.

When His time of ministry came, He continued to show Himself fully the opposite of Satan's rebellious pride and self-exaltation: "I honor My Father," He said; "If I glorify Myself, My glory is nothing" (John 8:49, 54).

Always the Victor

In every conflict with Satan and his evil spirits, Jesus came away as Victor. Even His disciples, through their Master's delegated authority, were able to vanquish strongholds of evil. After Jesus sent seventy of His followers out in ministry, they came back with joy and gave this report: "Lord, even the demons are subject to us in Your name." His response is powerful: "I was watching Satan fall from heaven like lightning. Behold, I have given you authority...over all the power of the enemy" (Luke 10:17–19). The unmistakable inference, according to J. Oswald Sanders, was that Christ's followers would also see the overthrow of Satan in their sphere of responsibility.

Finally the decisive battle raged at Calvary. It was Satan whom God used to bring this about; he had entered Judas's heart and prompted the idea of betraying Jesus. It appeared Satan was winning as Jesus submitted to capture, then torture, then crucifixion. He drew into Himself the sting of all sin and death and the utmost power of the enemy.

But through this apparent defeat, Jesus actually defeated the devil. He left Satan's forces humiliated and defenseless: "Having disarmed the powers and authorities, he made a public spectacle of them, triumphing over them by the cross" (Colossians 2:15, NIV). These foes became like bees without stingers, lions without teeth, snakes without fangs.

According to the world's values and estimation the Cross is only "weakness" (2 Corinthians 13:4; 1 Corinthians 1:23). It represents Christ's lack of self-assertion for His own rights. But from God's view, the Cross was a storming of the enemy's stronghold, death. On the cross Jesus invaded that stronghold, "that through death He might render powerless him who had power of death, that is, the devil" (Hebrews 2:14). He took away our enemy's biggest gun, his ultimate weapon, his greatest leverage over humanity—the power to keep people captive and condemned and dead in sin, separated from God through unpaid-for guilt.

What appeared to be the most horrible of all tragedies and Satan's greatest triumph was instead something God orchestrated into the Supreme Victory of all ages.

UNDER OUR FEET

Then came the final blow, as God exerted His unparalleled power and raised Jesus from the dead. Satan had been displayed as the venomous, hateful adversary of all that is good; in contrast, Christ, having entered Satan's stronghold of death, came away Victor—alive! "Up from the grave He arose, with a mighty triumph o'er His foes."

Now God has highly exalted Jesus, giving Him a name above all names, and awarding Him a position far above all the powers of Satan and his evil forces (Philippians 2:9–11; Ephesians 1:19–21).

And the amazing truth is that God has elevated us, spiritually, to the same exalted position Christ enjoys. God "raised us up with Him, and seated us

with Him in the heavenly places, in Christ Jesus"
(Ephesians 2:6). All the enemy powers are now under
our feet. As we take our stand in the victory of Christ,
Satan is powerless to defeat us.

We're not beneath our enemy, hoping against
hope that somehow we can overcome; in Christ we're
above Satan in the ultimate superior position. All the
advantages are on our side; all of them are found in the
person of the Lord Jesus Christ, who has already
overcome the worst Satan could do.

That's why Christ's victory is such an astounding
victory for you and me. When we turned by faith to
Him, His resurrection power was more than enough
to release us out of bondage into freedom—the
freedom of being right with God, liberated from guilt
and condemnation. We now stand in the benefits
which Christ's intense conflict and sweeping victory
have won. "God crossed out the whole debt against us
in His account books. He no longer counted the laws
we had broken. He nailed the account book to the
cross and closed the account" (Colossians 2:14,
Laubach).

Satan has no power to keep imprisoned those
who hear and respond to the message of Christ. Their
chains have been cut, their debt canceled. Satan has no

more authority to condemn the freed ones, or to demand any kind of payment.

Now God, through us, is continuing to bring this good news of release to people still held captive by the enemy. And He is setting the stage for Satan's final, utter defeat. May it be soon, Lord Jesus!

TWO

WHILE WE AWAIT THE KING

For still our ancient foe doth seek to work us woe;
His craft and power are great, and, armed with cruel hate,
On earth is not his equal.

The fatal blow has been dealt. The devil's authority has been broken. His eternal judgment is certain. He and his helpers will be removed and sentenced to the place of eternal flames and endless pain.

But that judgment has not yet been carried out. Although the pronouncement against him is irreversible, the sentence is yet to be enforced. And until the day of his final defeat, God allows him freedom to roam the earth.

Satan is still a roaring lion looking for people to tear apart and devour. He's still a skillful murderer and a shrewd liar who inflicts pain and tragedy and subtle deception on both non-Christians and true believers. He may try to do this personally, as he did with Jesus in His temptation, or he may do it through his legions of demonic helpers. He's alert to every invitation we unknowingly give him to do what he craves: to steal, to kill, to destroy.

But all this happens only under God's sovereignty and within set limits.

Satan is alive—but not well.

SATAN'S HOLD—HOW DEEP AND HOW WIDE?

When the devil tempted Jesus in the wilderness, he "showed him in an instant all the kingdoms of the world." Then he declared to God's Son, "I will give you all their authority and splendor, for it has been given to me, and I can give it to anyone I want to" (Luke 4:5–6, NIV). Was Satan exaggerating his abilities on that occasion and claiming more than he had a right to?

Jesus didn't give Satan the honor of arguing the point. His goal was not to debate Satan but to defeat his purpose—which He did, precisely and powerfully, by quoting from God's Word: "It is written: 'Man does not live on bread alone, but on every word that comes from the mouth of God'" (Matthew 4:4, NIV).

"The whole world lies in the power of the evil

one," the apostle John tells us (1 John 5:19). And Paul speaks of "the god of this world" who has blinded unbelievers' minds (2 Corinthians 4:4). But does this worldwide influence mean Satan is the undisputed ruler and sovereign of this earth, free to do whatever he wants in storms, earthquakes, and other natural calamities—or at least in sicknesses, trials, tragedies, accidents? Or does it primarily mean that people everywhere allow him supremacy in their lives by fitting in with his ways instead of God's?

Is Satan simply the source of "the lust of the flesh and the lust of the eyes and the boastful pride of life" (1 John 2:16), the bitter fountain from which such worldliness originates? Or is he even more than that? Some believers hold that anything less than God's perfect good in our lives should be directly attributed to Satan's pervasive and continuing acts. Yet I wonder, does this view make too much of Satan's rule and too little of God's?

When we blame Satan for all (or even most) of what goes wrong in a fallen world, we may too easily overlook God's sovereignty. We forget that "God is the King of all the earth" (Psalm 47:7). And we forget that Jesus addressed His Father as "Lord of heaven and earth" (Matthew 11:25).

As King and Judge and Ruler of the universe, God tells us, "I am the LORD, and there is no other, the One forming light and creating darkness, causing well-being and creating calamity; I am the LORD who does all these" (Isaiah 45:6–7). Light and well-being, yet also darkness and calamity—all go ultimately back to God. This passage (along with many others in the Word) deals a heavy blow to a simple dualism that neatly sorts and labels everything into two camps: the evil (all caused by Satan) and the good (all brought about by God).

Many Scriptures show God directly causing adverse circumstances. Take sickness for example. We learn in His Word that God is the giver of good health and that He loves to heal. Yet the Bible shows as well that He sends sickness at times. In Job's case He let Satan have a part in this, though even then He dictated just how far Satan could go. Moreover, people often bring sickness on themselves by not caring for their bodies, by choosing negative emotions and attitudes, or by more blatant sin—all coupled, aided, and abetted by viruses, bacteria, and toxins in our polluted world.

The awfulness of our human legacy through Adam is that we get what we deserve by nature and by choice. Death has spread in every generation like a malignant force, like faulty spiritual DNA. Belonging to the Lord doesn't automatically snatch us out of this "human condition" in a fallen world. But God is still in control. He often allows sickness—as well as weakness and sorrow—as opportunities in our lives to know Him better and glorify Him in new ways.

For years our daughter Doreen—mother of three young children—suffered from chronic fatigue syndrome. Was this disease imposed on her by Satan with God's permission, as Job's illness was? Or was it just an illness with purely natural causes? Whichever, God permitted it—and as with all our family's trials, it was part of our warfare between God's purposes and Satan's. God wanted to strengthen the faith of my daughter and her husband; Satan wanted to destroy it. God wanted to bring them forth as gold; Satan wanted to blur the image of Christ within them, to make them less like Him. God wanted to make them more effective for Him; Satan wanted to make them less effective.

The same higher truth applies to Satan's role as tempter: God will not let us be tempted beyond what we're able (1 Corinthians 10:13). We know that Satan's basic strategies center on spiritual and moral evil, yet can we attribute all moral evil to Satan? James traces our sin back to being carried away and enticed by our own lust (James 1:14–15). God doesn't blame sin on Satan, but holds every individual accountable. Satan may tempt—but we humans choose.

We must also remember that Satan is finite, not infinite. Nor is he present everywhere. He does have his servants far and wide—"huge numbers of wicked spirits in the spirit world" (Ephesians 6:12, TLB)—plus a highly effective communication system. Meanwhile he himself "prowls around" (1 Peter 5:8), and none of us knows how fast he can travel. But his range and capabilities cannot begin to compare with God's, or even with the power of His presence within a single believer: "Greater is He who is in you than he who is in the world" (1 John 4:4).

So we can blame too much on Satan; we can give him credit beyond his due. If we believe he has done something in our lives without God's permission, are we not in danger of making Satan greater than God? Perhaps God would like to tell us, "Blame it on Satan, you may; but see Me in it, you must."

God has Satan on a leash—a long leash, but nevertheless a leash. Satan is never entirely free to rampage through the world doing whatever he wants.

He's on a much longer leash when he deals with his own spiritual kingdom, the world system and the people in it. Yet in all things he is answerable to the One who has the whole world in His hand, the One who rides the heavens to care for His people and see that His plans are fulfilled (Deuteronomy 33:26).

That doesn't mean we should ever downplay the importance of the spiritual battle. We dare not neglect our role as part of Christ's army, engaged in direct and conscious battle against Satan and his works. But focusing too much on Satan and making too much of his works can cheat us, sometimes in subtle ways.

EVEN AT HIS WORST

To do his evil work against believers, Satan must ask permission, as we see when Jesus said to Peter, "Satan has asked permission to sift all of you like wheat" (Luke 22:31, Williams). With Job also, God wisely saw fit to give Satan permission to attack. He permits these attacks to test and refine us, to strengthen our faith, and to glorify Himself through us in new ways. He allows Satan to work, then He intervenes and delivers those who trust Him.

God has not in the least abdicated His throne.

His purposes are moving toward their ultimate completion. Their glorious fulfillment is advancing through His people today—and the gates of hell will not prevail against them. Whatever we may face from Satan and his hosts, we can always speak confidently to God the same words David spoke: "My times are in Your hand" (Psalm 31:15).

The Lion from the tribe of Judah, the Root of David, has overcome the lion who seeks to devour us. And as God shut the mouths of the lions for Daniel when he was thrown into their den, so also will He protect us in this world where the roaring lion and his accomplices roam. God's promise to those who will abide in the shadow of the Almighty includes this: "You shall tread upon the lion and the cobra, the young lion and the serpent you shall trample underfoot" (Psalm 91:13, NKJV).

The book of Revelation reveals Satan reaching the pinnacle of his role as God's adversary, through both human and demonic powers and through the Antichrist. Even then his actions will come only as God allows them. He will act under God's direct delegation of authority: "It was also given to him to make war with the saints and to overcome them, and authority over every tribe and people and tongue and nation was given to him" (Revelation 13:7). This authority will have a definite time limit set by God, as the book of Revelation also makes clear. Even when Satan is at his worst, he is still bound by the limitations set by God, his Creator.

All of Satan's schemes, all his dreams of lasting world domination, will end up giving glory to God. They will act as boomerangs, heightening Satan's ultimate disgrace and humiliation. Every taste of success he savors along the way will make his end more bitter. And after God's final victory, He will be able to say what He has been saying century after century as His plans come to pass: "Surely, just as I have intended so it has happened, and just as I have planned so it will stand.... For the LORD of hosts has planned, and who can frustrate it?" (Isaiah 14:24, 27).

MYSTERIES

Nevertheless, we serve a God of mystery, and this can often cause us to think "Why, Lord?" Our uncertainties can give the enemy opportunities to plant in us doubts, half-truths, or lies.

We understand that God is sovereign, so we wonder, "Why do the wicked flourish, and the righteous suffer?" This is not an easy question to answer. But we do know that God has set the wicked in slippery places and, in His time, will destroy them in a moment (Psalm 73:18–20). We also know that all the wicked of the earth must drink His cup of wrath— must drain it to the dregs (Psalm 92:7; 75:8). They want to get away with what they do and often they succeed—for a time.

An area of uncertainty and questioning in my life has stemmed from Jesus' statement that many people take the wide way leading to destruction, while only a few take the narrow way leading to life (Matthew 7:13–14). At times I've felt troubled and oppressed by this. It seems to grant the major victory to Satan. A part of me (and it's not the born-again part of me) prefers not to believe what Jesus says here. It's easier to think that somehow all will eventually be saved. Now and then a stabbing doubt, a flaming missile, pierces my heart and mind. It doesn't seem *possible* that the vast majority will choose to stay in Satan's kingdom and will end up excluded forever from God's glory, with thirst that will never be quenched. It's more comfortable to think that somehow we've misread the Bible, that this is not what God has actually said.

This "part of me" that sends up these doubts is

my inner traitor—my "flesh," the sin nature which indwells me, the part of me that is Satan's ally. So I've learned to quickly choose against these lies, silencing them with praise that God's Word is true—and if necessary, with specific Scriptures on eternal punishment.

Emotionally I might like to get around this statement from Jesus by some sort of mental gymnastics, by finding texts here and there that seem to counterbalance Jesus' statement. But inner release comes by another route. It simply isn't true that Satan will end up with a greater kingdom than Christ's. Satan will end up in utter shame and disgrace. And if he has any semblance of kingdom rule throughout eternity, it will be over God-resisting nobodies— people who were granted free choice, who chose "nothingness," and who have gotten what they chose. And their "god," Satan, who deceived them, will be suffering bitterness, defeat, slavery, and the misery of unfulfilled ambition forever.

Meanwhile, as the history of this age continues, thousands of people—millions—are being saved and released to a life of allegiance to Christ, now and forever. God's growing church may be composed mainly of the small ones of the earth (1 Corinthians

1:27), unacclaimed and despised by the "great" and the "wise." But to them the invisible glory has already been granted, and for all eternity they will reign as glorious beings. And there will be no comparison between their combined "weight of glory" and the shame, the nothingness, of Satan and of all who have chosen against eternal life!

For now, this can sometimes be hard to grasp. But relating to a God we don't fully understand is a bit like relating to a computer and its maker. I'm not a computer expert, and my computer is a mystery to me in countless ways. But if I do what the makers and experts say, my little computer does me a lot of good. And if someone infects it with a virus, I don't blame the company that made it.

God has given us answers. He has spelled out broad principles which sometimes don't make sense from a time-bound, earth-bound point of view. But they do reassure the heart that honors Him as God, refusing to impose its own small framework on Him. Such a person understands and knows and loves Him. And true love reveals an understanding spirit even when we don't understand. So we're never to sit in judgment of God, blaming Him for not taking action. We're not to put Him in the little black box of our understanding. Instead we're to sit at His feet as learners.

God has established His credibility. We can see this by taking a long look at Bible history. His wisdom is trustworthy: "Oh, the depth of the riches both of the wisdom and knowledge of God! How unsearchable are His judgments and unfathomable His ways! For who has known the mind of the Lord, or who became His counselor? Or who has first given to Him that it might be paid back to him again? For from Him and through Him and to Him are all things. To Him be the glory forever. Amen" (Romans 11:33–36).

We can resolve our uncertainties only by considering the heart of God revealed in the Scriptures and at the Cross. He is just, loving, good, and wise. There is no human way to understand the ways of life God has planned. He has in mind incredible glory and enrichment forever for countless believers—infinitely beyond the best utopia we might dream up. And He relates to all people with full fairness, full justice, incredible expressions of love, and the offer of relationship with Himself—not wanting any to align with the enemy against Him, but allowing this if people refuse Him.

The pivotal battle in God's war (and ours) against Satan has been won; the outcome is absolutely sure. Meanwhile, although the whole war is under the sovereign supervision of the supreme God, yet the outcome of each of our battles and skirmishes is not certain. We can choose defeats.

Each trial we face is part of the warfare. Some battles are short. We take our stand with early, visible triumph. Other trials stretch on and on as the enemy keeps sniping at us, throwing fiery darts again and again, seeking to wear us down. As we persevere with our eyes on God even in prolonged trials, the Spirit of glory and of God rests upon us (1 Peter 4:14). So having done all, we must keep standing.

Satan is shrewd, his strategies are demonic, and his power is ominous. Yet we must keep in mind that he is a defeated enemy. Behind the fierce growls, behind the show of strength, he cringes—not before us, but before the One who by His death and resurrection has conquered him and sealed his fate.

We stand on the firm ground of who our Victor is and all that He has done.

How Much Should
We Know?

The prince of darkness grim, we tremble not for him;
His rage we can endure, for lo, his doom is sure:
One little word shall fell him.

In battling Satan and his demons, it's not easy
to maintain a scriptural balance and avoid
excesses. Satan is delighted if we ignore him and let him
do his evil work unhindered. But if we get serious about
his defeat, he tempts us to exaggerate his power and
become absorbed with him and his helpers, giving them
the limelight they delight in. Or he gets us sidetracked
into speculations and unscriptural practices.

It's not easy to maintain an awareness of Satan
and demons without letting them become a major
emphasis of our life and ministry. We all need prayer
for proper balance in this.

FICTION OR FACT?

Our world abounds with information about the devil.
And how easy it is to base our beliefs about Satan and

our dealings with him on experiences we hear about that may not be scriptural. Or on what demons themselves tell people, as though they can be trusted. Or on novels that stimulate us to pray and resist Satan, but at the same time, as vivid and gripping fiction, go beyond what the Word teaches into conjecture, suppositions, and fantasy.

I rejoice that God has used such novels. They bring a heightened awareness that we're engaged in a spiritual war against crafty, powerful enemies, that victory is possible through Christ, and that each of us can help assure victory as we pray and resist Satan. Yet I feel concerned for those who may be left terrified whenever they pass a shadowy bush or dark corner. For decades to come, many Christians may base much of their doctrine of spiritual warfare on imaginary descriptions, failing to discern what is scriptural and what is speculative.

Take, for example, the current emphasis on "territorial" spirits. Some overseas missionaries have invested much time and attention trying to find out the names and ranks of local demons, and especially the names of high-ranking demons in charge of large regions or entire countries. It's as though God cannot answer prayer and defeat the enemy as we simply keep praying in faith, binding Satan and his hierarchy of helpers regardless of their names or their ranks. Does it matter that a nation may have six territorial spirits—or two or nine? The pagans may fear and worship what they call territorial spirits, but this doesn't prove that such spirits are in fact what they claim to be. After all, they represent the father of lies!

Satan is actively at work in every nation, and we must be committed to his defeat. But are large amounts of information about the enemy necessary, or even advisable?

THE DEEP THINGS OF SATAN

The Word gives simple, concrete facts about the enemy. Now and then God lifts the curtain just a bit, giving us behind-the-scenes glimpses. These glimpses can motivate us to pray against Satan and the powerful spiritual rulers of his domain. We see this in the book of Job, where Satan appears before God. And in Daniel 10, we meet one of God's heavenly warriors. From him we learn that at least some nations (such as Persia and Greece) have had a special evil "prince," a powerful satanic angel. The "prince of Persia" was seeking to hinder God's answers to Daniel's prayer and prevent God's great prophetic message about the last times. This passage also shows that God has His own angelic princes—Michael, Israel's prince, being one of the chief (verse 21). Daniel 12:1 refers again to Michael, and calls him "the great prince who stood guard" over Israel.

But even in such fascinating passages, the Lord chose to reveal very few details. He lets us know there are powerful angelic princes, both evil and good. But how many? Which ones are over which nations? God has not revealed this. Nor did Daniel, as he prayed, need to know who was fighting whom, or even that evil spirits were involved. He prayed effectively without even knowing what was going on in the invisible battle between good and evil forces. As far as we know, the Lord never told him the names of these demonic rulers. Yet his prayers were highly effective.

We too can pray simply against our spiritual enemies and their purposes, even as David did against his physical enemies in Psalm 143:8–12—"Let me hear Your lovingkindness in the morning; for I trust in You; teach me the way in which I should walk.... Deliver me, O LORD, from my enemies.... Let Your good Spirit lead me on level ground.... And in Your lovingkindness, cut off my enemies and destroy all those who afflict my soul, for I am Your servant." God is certain to know exactly which spiritual enemies are involved against us, and He'll understand the best way to fend them off.

Jesus never commanded us to find out secret things about the enemy. Instead He commanded us to preach the gospel and make disciples. And though Paul made mention of "principality and power and might and dominion," we have no indication that he knew or cared about the exact pecking order of satanic forces. His emphasis was on Christ's exalted position high above all the forces of evil. And he stressed our being strong in the Lord, putting on the whole armor of God, praying for all saints and being bold in proclaiming the gospel (Ephesians 1:20–21, NKJV; 6:10–20).

Actually, the Bible contains relatively little information on the devil. The Lord even warns against learning the so-called "deep things of Satan" (Revelation 2:24). And in Deuteronomy 29:29 we read, "The secret things belong to the LORD our God, but the things revealed belong to us and to our sons forever, that we may observe all the words of this law." We need to be cautious about going "beyond what is written" (1 Corinthians 4:6, NIV), and we need to rely on the Holy Spirit to help us carefully test information about the enemy. "The Spirit searches all things, yes, the deep things of God" (1 Corinthians 2:10, NKJV). Make sure that new revelations and experiences (your own or other people's) are the deep things of God through the Holy Spirit, not the deep things of Satan.

FOUR

OPEN CONFRONTATION

And though this world, with devils filled,
should threaten to undo us,
We will not fear, for God hath willed
His truth to triumph through us.

 Some Christian leaders who emphasize warfare against Satan are in vital touch with what is happening in our society and have a deep desire to deliver people who have been ensnared by Satan. Their beliefs about the kingdom of God encourage a heavy stress on warring against Satan and casting out demons.

Some are committed to an essentially "Satanward" view of Scripture which lends extreme importance to Jesus' coming to destroy the works of the devil in people's lives. They see this as His all-inclusive purpose. This view of Scripture tends to see the Church almost solely as the army of God continuing the battle Jesus began against these works of Satan. Much emphasis is given to our conducting spiritual warfare through "power encounters" with the enemy, "power evangelism," and miraculous "signs and wonders."

Does this approach make us more effective in our spiritual warfare? Or might it to some degree be a diversionary strategy that Satan uses?

We can overestimate our responsibility or misdirect our efforts regarding Satan, and become so primed by aggressive models that we end up confrontive and combative. It's easy for us to overlook the example of Michael the archangel, who while disputing with the devil "did not pronounce against him a railing judgment," but instead put the matter into God's hands by saying, "The Lord rebuke you" (Jude 1:9).

It appears from the book of Acts that when Paul entered a new city or region, he wasn't focused on directly confronting evil powers, pagan worship, and superstitious beliefs. Christ and Him crucified was Paul's message. Often "signs and wonders" did not take place until after his initial thrust with the gospel. Signs and wonders in fact are never spoken of in Scripture as weapons of warfare.

"Power evangelism" to Paul seems to have centered in the power of the gospel, with the Spirit's conviction. He emphasized that "the word of the cross" is "the power of God" (1 Corinthians 1:18), and he reminded the Corinthian believers, "I determined to know nothing among you except Jesus Christ, and Him crucified" (1 Corinthians 2:2).

EXPELLING DEMONS

Especially prominent today is a focus on expelling demons.

Knowing how to battle against demonic activity has always been important, but perhaps in our day this is more important than ever—especially in the West, where we see a menacing flood of demonic activity.

Missionaries in many parts of the world have long practiced demon expulsions as the need has arisen. Many people have been released from terrible bondage because God has led some of His servants to pore over the Scriptures on the subject of spiritual warfare and put in practice what He has taught them. The need for this in the West may continue to escalate in the coming years. It could be that if more of God's servants expelled demons now and then in the course of their ministry, the heavy load of this work would not fall on a few. Though this is not a task to be taken on lightly without the Lord's clear leading, there is a need for spiritual, mature Christians, nourished in the

Word—pastors and missionaries as well as godly laymen—who can cast out demons when necessary.

Yet, though demon activity seems to be on the increase, we do not find support in God's Word for "tuning in to the spirit world" as some say, and becoming almost engrossed with expelling evil spirits. In some cases there seems to be almost a fixation on demons. The Lord's servants get so involved in delving deeper into a knowledge and understanding of evil spirits that time alone with the Lord and even adequate rest fall by the wayside, and disciples tend to become Satan-centered.

Moreover, the demons themselves seem to relish all the attention. Sometimes they flock to ministries that give them excessive attention (like Satan, their master, they love the limelight). But when such ministries refocus on Christ and His major, worldwide purposes, demons seem to lose interest and seek out other opportunities.

JESUS AND DEMONS

In the ministry of Jesus recorded in the Gospels, He was quick to help those who came to Him wanting deliverance from demons for themselves or their loved ones. His weapon in casting them out was simply His spoken word—the sword of the Spirit. However, He did not seem to be on a crusade looking for demons to cast out.

Note, for example, his response to Judas (in John 13:26–27). When Satan came into Judas, Jesus did not confront the demon, but said, "Now is the Son of Man glorified." Jesus was not taken by surprise; it was part of the Father's plan. Jesus was outmaneuvering the devil. In fact, when He chose Judas, He knew from the beginning that he would betray Him (John 6:64–65).

Casting out demons was not the major or even the central part of Jesus' ministry, for His focus was on something essentially higher and more positive: "For this cause I have come into the world, that I should bear witness to the truth" (John 18:37, NKJV).

The Apostles and Demons

The book of Acts gives us only a few instances of demon expulsion. We read of three special times of physical healing, and these occasions also included unclean spirits coming out of people. This took place through Peter and the apostles in Jerusalem (Acts 5:16), through Philip in Samaria (Acts 8:7), and through Paul in Ephesus (Acts 19:12).

Although Paul took the gospel into pagan cultures where demonic religions and the occult were rampant, he did not seek a broad ministry of casting out demons. He did not seem to be always on the alert for opportunities to confront and challenge satanic forces. Instead he was preoccupied with a deliverance ministry that was more basic and positive—"the ministry which I received from the Lord Jesus, to testify to the gospel of the grace of God" (Acts 20:24, NKJV).

If anything, he seemed to proceed in the area of casting out demons with a degree of caution. We see this in Acts 16:16–18, where Luke relates a rather puzzling event that occurred in Philippi. A slave girl who had a spirit of divination followed Paul and his band for many days, crying out their identity. Finally Paul, greatly annoyed, cast the demon out of her. It seems clear that Paul's obsession was to proclaim Christ, and that casting out demons was not a major goal.

This same lack of emphasis on demons is reflected throughout the New Testament epistles as well. Judging then by the entire New Testament, casting out demons would seem to be a relatively small part of our overall spiritual warfare.

Are we to seek "power encounters" with evil spirits? Are we to eagerly grab the opportunity to confront demons through a "deliverance ministry"?

Actually, all of us are already called to a deliverance ministry—to do our part in delivering unbelievers through the gospel and to help deliver Christians through such things as discipling, counseling, witnessing, teaching, and on and on.

A few of us may be called to a "deliverance ministry" that focuses directly against Satan. But even in this mission, casting out demons is probably a relatively small part. More important is a deep understanding that our solid basis for defeating Satan and his demons is our Lord Jesus Christ and basic truths about Him—His death and resurrection, His ascended position far above enemy powers, His blood, His name that is far above every name in every age. For believers who may face demonic attack, we must help them renounce anything from their past that might give Satan a toehold in their lives, and help them understand that their position in Christ is already far above all enemy powers. We must help them learn how to be filled with the Holy Spirit, to be strong in the Lord and to put on the armor He has provided—and especially to understand the power and authority of God's Word in facing our enemies.

Some years ago I was meeting regularly with a Japanese-American girl named Betty who had been brought up in a spiritist family. Though by then Betty was a mature Christian, she found herself severely oppressed by evil spirits whenever she went home for a visit. I helped Betty do a thorough Bible study on the truth that Jesus is Victor. Our study placed far more emphasis on the Lord than on the enemy. Betty learned to hold up the shield of faith in times of enemy attack, and began to use specific Scriptures as her sword, such as Colossians 2:15, Ephesians 1:19–20, and 1 John 4:4. The next time she went home, she experienced complete release from any sense of oppression.

A missionary family we knew in Southeast Asia was living in a house where demonic activity terrified their young son at night. They completely dispelled this satanic influence by reading aloud the Word of God in the areas of the house involved.

Warren and a fellow missionary once learned at a conference that a rather new Christian there, Mei Ling (not her real name), was being oppressed by a demon. Night after night she would wake up terrified as the demon sought to choke her; her Christian roommate reported that whenever this happened she could hear Mei Ling struggling to breathe. The two girls had prayed, but there was no improvement.

Warren and his coworker suggested that Mei Ling select one of the Scriptures she had memorized—one that seemed especially appropriate—and begin quoting it out loud as soon as she felt the demon grasping her throat. About six months later we learned that Mei Ling was doing this and that the attacks were far less frequent. Some time later her roommate informed us that the deliverance was complete, with no more demonic attacks. Not only was Mei Ling delivered, but she had learned much about resisting the devil. And though the experience was traumatic, the demon was not able to actually harm the girl or destroy her faith.

I could tell many other stories that demonstrate the power and protection Christ provides for us against demons.

About A.D. 150, Justin Martyr wrote of there being "numberless demoniacs throughout the whole world," and of "many of our Christian men exorcizing them in the Name of Jesus Christ." Though we see no scriptural precedent for making demon expulsion a major theme or a commonplace practice, yet I pray for more men like those Justin Martyr described—men who will confront enemy powers and cast out demons without getting into any of the questionable beliefs and practices that are so plentiful in our day.

FIVE

OUR BEST RESISTANCE

We rest on Thee, our Shield and our Defender!
Thine is the battle, Thine shall be the praise;
When passing through the gates of pearly splendor,
Victors, we rest with Thee, through endless days.

Satan's strategy and tactics flow from his character. Jesus has told us that Satan "was a murderer from the beginning, and does not stand in the truth because there is no truth in him. Whenever he speaks a lie, he speaks from his own nature, for he is a liar and the father of lies" (John 8:44). Above all else, he is a murderer and a liar, the sworn enemy of both life and truth. In his murderous and destructive intent, he uses lies as his foremost weapon—lies that are deadly. With those lies he wants to deceive and devour us—to destroy our vitality and usefulness.

A LOOK AT HIS LIES

Satan wants to get us to do and to be the opposite of whatever God approves and delights in.

As he tries to accomplish this, his basic method is to deceive us—to get us to embrace false convictions about God, about salvation, about ourselves and our identity, about how life runs well. Satan is a fraud, and he festoons his deceptions with enticing promises of freedom and fulfillment. But everything he offers is a sham.

He especially seeks to deceive believers by getting them sidetracked from grace—from the good news of grace and of salvation in its present tense as well as its past tense. He gets us to rely on our own merits and efforts. He speaks lies that get us centered in ourselves and how well we're doing instead of in Christ and all He has done and is doing. Just as the serpent deceived Eve by his craftiness, so our enemy is seeking to lead our minds astray from the simplicity and purity of devotion to Christ (2 Corinthians 11:3).

He also maneuvers to get us conformed to this world, not just in worldly pleasures but also in fearing what they fear, in being anxious, in seeking what they seek and grasping for the same things they grasp for.

Satan is subtle and sly. If he can't get us into obvious evil or heresy, he'll try to allure us into whatever is the next worst—or the next or the next.

He tries to sidetrack us into some sort of "good"

primary focus other than Christ. And a "spiritual" primary focus will do as well as a fleshly one. He prods us to be centered on performance, deliverance, disciplines, spiritual excitement, feelings, people—anything that may be good in its place but that was never meant to be primary; anything that is prone to become a lust, a craving, a major distraction.

One of Satan's titles is the accuser of the brothers (and sisters). And one of his chief strategies—one he's at day and night—is to accuse and discredit us. Job 1 and 2 let us in on this constant scene of accusation.

In keeping with all this deception, Satan likes to disguise himself as an angel of light, pretending to be what he was before he rebelled. Meanwhile his agents—false teachers—likewise disguise themselves, masquerading as servants of Christ (2 Corinthians 11:13–15).

How do we resist?

Satan, the prince of darkness, hates light. Light repels him. So we are to cast off the works of darkness and put on the armor of light. We're to put on the Lord Jesus Christ, the One who is Light, who is altogether righteous, and who is Victor over the deeds and powers of darkness (Romans 13:14). In Him we have become "Light in the Lord," able to repel Satan by living and acting as children of light (Ephesians 5:8).

We need to search the Scriptures daily to see if we have let secondary things become idols—if in any way we've been led away from being Christ centered— if Satan is using attractive "good" things to allure us away from the priorities the Lord has for us.

We're able to overcome Satan by the blood of the Lamb and by the truth we proclaim (Revelation 12:11)—much as the blood on the doorposts that first Passover repelled the death angel. The blood is not a magical charm or incantation or formula. The blood represents our Lord's redemptive work on the cross. And the Lamb slain is now the Lamb glorified and exalted. So we overcome by counting on the death and resurrection and glorious position of our Lord, far above all evil powers.

OUR POSITIVE CALLING

In the universal war with Satan that has raged for ages, we may sometimes think we don't even "count" in the spiritual battles unless we're consciously and directly warring against Satan.

But our main calling is to God and His positive purposes in our lives, our witness, and all of our service. This positive focus helps defeat Satan; it lifts up and honors God, which is the last thing Satan wants to have happen. We continually bring defeat to Satan as we live in the marvelous grace that God has lavished on us—as we more and more experience victory and freedom.

On the whole, our warfare is focused on glorious, positive goals. It means fulfilling God's longings to call out a people for Himself, a vast family of children who will be conformed to the image of His Son. It means fulfilling His desire for an army of soldiers whose main task is to make known, by life and by word, the good news of the reconciled life, the transformed life, and the conquering life.

Our being involved in fulfilling these longings of God's heart automatically defeats Satan and his purposes. Whatever we do that glorifies the Lord helps defeat Satan.

Have you noticed what a large percentage of the Lord's commands relate to positive Christian virtues, compared to His commands regarding Satan? Learning and obeying His commands always represents a positive thrust in fulfilling His glorious purposes—and this strikes a piercing blow against Satan and what he wants.

Therefore in seeking to defeat Satan and his strategies, let's be obsessed with the glory of God. Surely this is the best, the most pointed rebuff we can give the enemy, for it is directly opposed to what he longs for. "Whatever you do in word or deed, do all in the name of the Lord Jesus, giving thanks through Him to God the Father" (Colossians 3:17). "Whether, then, you eat or drink or whatever you do, do all to the glory of God" (1 Corinthians 10:31).

STARTLING POWER

The main Bible passage on how to resist Satan is Ephesians 6:10–18. Here the Lord gives us a foundation for our beliefs about spiritual warfare, as well as powerful weapons we can use in battle.

Other helpful Scriptures on the vast resources of His power are Ephesians 1:19–22 and 3:20. These inspiring passages describe the power of God that is available to us—the same power He used to raise Christ from the dead and enthrone Him in the heavenly realms, high above all other powers—power that can do infinitely more than we can ask or dream of.

In *The Christ Crowned,* S. D. Gordon writes of "the startling, revolutionary power, softly, subtly, but with resistless sweep, flowing down from the crowned Christ, among grateful men." And all of that power, he reminds us, is at the disposal of any disciple of Christ—even the humblest—who will simply live in full-faced touch with Him, and who will take of that power as the need comes, and as the sovereign Holy Spirit leads.

These power passages in Ephesians became especially meaningful for Warren and me when our son Brian was taken captive by Satan the year he turned eighteen. It wasn't Satan worship or the occult. It wasn't drugs or sex. Instead, he was trapped in existentialism, agnosticism, and nihilism—modern philosophies that drive many young people to commit suicide.

This ushered us into one of our longest, most traumatic periods of spiritual warfare. As years crept by, God used truths from His Word to rescue us from fear and unbelief—two ways Satan likes to cripple us. How grateful we were for those passages in Ephesians showing us the Lord's vast resources and power which are available to us in resisting Satan.

As we prayed for Brian, we focused on many other Scriptures as well, verses that stimulated our faith as we turned them into praise and thanksgiving. Often we would thank the Lord for permitting this trial and praise Him that in His time He would work it for Brian's good and the good of many others. We often went back to Psalm 66:3, reminding ourselves that God's awesome power is so great that His enemies cringe before Him. We also found much strength in Jeremiah 32:17—"Ah, Lord GOD! Behold, You have made the heavens and the earth by Your great power and by Your outstretched arm! Nothing is too difficult for You."

Perhaps the most helpful verse was Isaiah 49:25 "Surely, thus says the LORD, 'Even the captives of the mighty man will be taken away, and the prey of the tyrant will be rescued; for I will contend with the one who contends with you, and I will save your sons.'" How thankful we were that we could apply this verse about Israel's earthly warfare to Brian's spiritual struggles.

Although we were twelve thousand miles away from Brian at the time, we had access to God's throne room, and God had access to Brian. After about five years the Lord delivered him, and he has become a godly pastor who is deep in the Word and prayer.

SECRET OF STRENGTH

"Put on the full armor of God," Paul tells us, "so that you can take your stand against the devil's schemes.

For our struggle is not against flesh and blood, but against the rulers, against the authorities, against the powers of this dark world and against the spiritual forces of evil in the heavenly realms." (Ephesians 6:11–12, NIV). Our King has supplied armor for our spiritual wrestling that the enemy cannot pierce with any of his weapons or strategies.

But before Paul exhorts us to put on this armor, he says, "Finally, be strong in the Lord and in His mighty power" (Ephesians 6:10, NIV). In warring against our powerful spiritual enemies, mere human strength cannot succeed. This is true when our wrestling takes the form of resisting temptation or overcoming obstacles in our service; it's also true when it takes the form of praying and binding Satan by faith.

We learn what the Lord's strength and might are like in Ephesians 1:19–22 (NIV), where Paul prayed that the believers might know "his incomparably great power for us who believe. That power is like the working of his mighty strength, which he exerted in Christ when he raised him from the dead and seated him at his right hand in the heavenly realms, far above all rule and authority, power and dominion, and every title that can be given, not only in the present age but also in the one to come. And God placed all things under his feet...." It's in our union with this almighty Person and His invincible power that we're to be strong.

How does the Lord infuse this power into us? Again we find the answer in Paul's prayers, this time in Ephesians 3:16–17 (NIV)—"that out of his glorious riches he may strengthen you with power through his Spirit in your inner being, so that Christ may dwell in your hearts through faith." Not little dribbles of power grudgingly doled out, but "according to the riches of His glory" (v. 16, NASB). Not the power of a dynamic personality or the power of human wisdom and intrigue and scheming and carefully worked-out methods, but spiritual power through the Holy Spirit as we let Him fill us. Power that is made perfect through weakness, power that comes by grace through faith in the One who "is able to do far more abundantly beyond all that we ask or think, according to the power that works within us" (Ephesians 3:20). High-voltage spiritual power that makes the enemy cringe!

These prayers of Paul tell us much about warfare praying for ourselves and others. Through praying over the Scriptures we can absorb the reality of how great our Lord's power is, and we can experience it more fully in our inner person through the Spirit. Sometimes our prayer can be simple, believing prayer; sometimes it must be wrestling in prayer as the enemy seeks to undermine our faith or that of others.

Being strong in the Lord involves the choice, the daily and hourly choice, not to rely on our own powers but on the strength and power of His might, of His Spirit. "Not that we are sufficient of ourselves...but our sufficiency is from God" (2 Corinthians 3:5, NKJV). "Is"—not will be, but now is! "We are powerless before this great multitude who are coming against us; nor do we know what to do, but our eyes are on You" (2 Chronicles 20:12).

All the Armor, Always

All the pieces of armor in Ephesians 6:13–17 symbolize the reality of God and the redemptive work of Christ; and taking them up means experiencing them in our daily lives. It means keeping them in the forefront of our consciousness by meditating often on what they mean and depending on the Holy Spirit to enlighten and enable us.

Whatever approach we find useful, it is crucial

that we make sure that each thing represented by the pieces of armor is a current reality in our lives: truth...righteousness...the gospel and the peace it brings...faith...salvation (including present and future salvation)...and the Word. And as a basis for all these we must be strong in the Lord and in His mighty power (v. 10). In other words, the armor in Ephesians 6 represents a life that is responsive to the context of this passage.

Paul says elsewhere, "Let us cast off the works of darkness, and let us put on the armor of light" (Romans 13:12, NKJV). Our armor is not made of stiff metal; rather it's like light itself, shining and bright and weightless.

Paul tells us to put on the *whole* armor. So these armor pieces are not isolated qualities Christians should have. They are interrelated; they affect one another. We can't pick and choose among them, ignoring some while we have others fully in place.

For example, our helmet of salvation—past, present, and future salvation—relates to peace and righteousness as well as hope. God also links righteous living with joy and peace. And all of them are linked with being strong in the Lord—in a blend of cause and effect, for we are strong by faith (Hebrews 11). But our spiritual strength leaks away if we neglect cultivating our faith. Then we're left merely with human strength, which is of no use in this war against mighty spiritual powers who are evil through and through. And even our human strength can drain away when we sin by neglecting some piece of armor. "When I kept silent about my sin," David says, "...my vitality was drained away" (Psalm 32:3–4).

Furthermore, taking up this armor is not something we're to do only when we sense danger or feel attacked or oppressed. We're not to suddenly dash for the armor when the battle gets fierce. Rather, it's the way we're to live all the time, because we are in fact in danger; we are in a war. Our enemy is sly and sneaky and often comes upon us when we least expect it. Our life is like driving through a high-crime neighborhood where a bulletproof car would be in order, or like crossing a field planted with mines and ringed by snipers. The armor is ours for day and night protection, as well as for times of intense temptation or attack. And it's an invisible kind of armor that we can even sleep in comfortably.

Wearing our armor all the time has to do with experiencing God day by day and choosing continually to live in obedience. It means choosing to live a life that is a constant affront to our spiritual enemy, a life that continually cuts across his purposes, a life that draws people away from him, making them dissatisfied with his domain.

Always wearing the armor won't keep us from being attacked, but it will keep us safe whenever an attack comes.

AND FINALLY, PRAYER

Paul tops off this passage about spiritual warfare in Ephesians 6 by pointing out the vital need for warfare praying: "And pray in the Spirit on all occasions with all kinds of prayers and requests. With this in mind, be alert and always keep on praying for all the saints" (Ephesians 6:18, NIV).

This is not a postscript or an afterthought, for prayer is a key to effective wrestling against our mighty spiritual enemies. We see this prayer-wrestling in Paul's great struggle as he interceded for the Colossians, as well as in Epaphras's earnest labor for them in prayer (Colossians 2:1–3; 4:12).

Praying in the Spirit includes being empowered by the Holy Spirit and prompted by Him to pray according to what He has written in His Word. He never leads us to pray contrary to His Word, which He Himself inspired.

Through praise and prayer we can then, like a guerrilla unit, penetrate enemy territory. We have no need to be afraid of Satan, though he is out to disable us. Satan is afraid of *us* as we rely on our resources in Christ.